Succeeding with
Your L

Succeeding with Your Literature Review

A handbook for students

Paul Oliver

Open University Press

Open University Press
McGraw-Hill Education
McGraw-Hill House
Shoppenhangers Road
Maidenhead
Berkshire
England
SL6 2QL

email: enquiries@openup.co.uk
world wide web: www.openup.co.uk

and Two Penn Plaza, New York, NY 10121-2289, USA

First published 2012

A catalogue record of this book is available from the British Library

ISBN-13: 978-0-33-524368-6
ISBN-10: 0-33-524368-1
eISBN: 978-0-33-524369-3

Library of Congress Cataloging-in-Publication Data
CIP data applied for

Typesetting and e-book compilations by
RefineCatch Limited, Bungay, Suffolk
Printed in the UK by Bell & Bain Ltd, Glasgow

Fictitious names of companies, products, people, characters and/or
data that may be used herein (in case studies or in examples) are not
intended to represent any real individual, company, product or event.

The **McGraw·Hill** Companies

Contents

Introduction

The literature review is one of the most important parts of any piece of academic writing. It is rather like the foundations upon which the rest of the work is built. Bricklayers never start building a house until a solid concrete foundation, with all the drainpipes, has been laid first. Once the foundation is laid, they can connect the rest of the house to it. In a similar way, all academic writing needs a base on which it can be fixed. A literature review provides a sound base upon which new research can be founded. Later, further research will be added, and the building will get taller and taller. If each stage is done properly, the building will not fall down!

People often say that there is nothing new in the world – that all apparently new knowledge is based at least partly, upon previous knowledge. In any subject area, the literature review provides that previous knowledge, and gives us an anchor to which to attach our new ideas. Researching and writing a good literature review is not, however, an easy task. This requires careful thought and planning, a clear structure, analytic thinking, extremely good information search skills, the ability to synthesize and summarize information in a clear writing style, and the ability to integrate this with the rest of your research work. There are a lot of important skills here!

It is rarely, if ever, possible to just sit down and write a literature review. This is what makes it such a demanding task, and one which many students find somewhat difficult. Before you can ever start writing the actual literature review, you will need to assemble a large quantity of information. You will then need to classify this literature, and perhaps reject some of it. After reading it initially, you will then divide it into sections, ready for discussion and analysis. All of this has to be done before you put your pen to paper, and it is the sheer amount of work involved which can tend to be rather frustrating for students. You quite naturally want to get on as quickly as possible with writing the chapter, but feel that you have to slow down and take things more slowly. You will need to read articles, book chapters and internet materials very carefully, examining ways in which different pieces of literature might be related. This can be so demanding, that it can seem to hold you back from the 'real' job of writing the dissertation. I hope that this book will explain in more detail why a literature review is so important, and will also give you a range of strategies to help you write it more efficiently and effectively.

Most students in higher education have to write a literature review as part of a piece of work, although typically it is associated with a dissertation. This can be during the final year of an undergraduate course, as the final piece of work for a Masters degree, or as the main piece of work for a doctorate. Some of you may also be writing an article, with a view to getting it published in an academic journal. In all these cases, you will need to write a literature review. Perhaps surprisingly, the process of researching and writing a literature review does not differ very much between the main different levels in higher education. Whether you are at undergraduate or doctoral level, you still have to decide on the types of literature to review; you have to find examples of that literature, and select suitable quotations; and then you have to analyze the items of literature, and produce a coherent discussion. You should find that most of the advice and techniques described in this book are relevant to any level in higher education. However, there are one or two issues which are specific to, say, undergraduate or doctoral level. Perhaps the most obvious is the relative length of the literature review. At undergraduate or Masters levels, the literature review for a dissertation may typically be 2000 or 3000 words in length. A doctoral thesis may often be about 80,000 words long, however, and the literature review at least 20,000 words, and maybe more.

These differences in length can have an effect on the way in which you approach the review. If you have to write a long review, then you will need to select a subject for your research, on which quite a lot has been written. If the subject has not attracted a lot of writers, then you may find it difficult to fulfil the required length of the review, or on the other hand, you may need to include some less-relevant literature. A long literature review, such as occurs in a doctoral dissertation, will also require much more discussion, analysis and synthesis than in, say, an undergraduate dissertation. In the book, where there are issues which relate to a literature review at a particular academic level, these are indicated.

The structure of the book also includes a number of features which should help you navigate through it. Each chapter has a summary at the beginning, along with learning outcomes, which should help you plan your learning before reading the full chapter. At the end of the chapter is a list of some key terms which occur in the chapter, along with an explanation of their meaning. These key terms are highlighted where they first occur in the chapter. There is also a list of key questions at the end of the chapter which can help you check what you have learned. Each chapter ends with a short list of key readings, to help you develop your literature review further.

In the main body of each chapter are a number of highlighted boxes which emphasize certain points of interest. In each chapter there is also a 'good practice' box and a 'common pitfall' box. The former suggests ideas or approaches which you might find helpful in producing a good literature review, while the latter mentions mistakes or less desirable approaches. Overall, it is worth remembering that writing a literature review, or indeed writing anything, is a creative activity. Guide books such as this can point the way, help you get started, and provide advice while you are working. But at the end of the day, a good piece of writing is created by you, by applying your own intellect and unique insights. Ultimately, that is what will make your literature review very special!

1

The nature and purpose of a literature review

Summary

A literature review is usually regarded as being an essential part of student projects, research studies and dissertations. This chapter examines the reasons for the importance of the literature review, and the things which it tries to achieve. It also explores the main strategies which you can use to write a good literature review.

Learning outcomes

After reading this chapter you should be able to do the following:

- Understand the nature of a literature review.
- Summarize the reasons why a literature review is regarded as being so important in projects and dissertations.

- List and understand the main ways in which you can go about reviewing a body of literature.

The nature of a literature review

Just about every student has at one time or another had to write a literature review! However, despite the fact that it is almost obligatory in research studies and dissertations, there is often not the time on busy courses for tutors to devote all the time to it that the subject deserves. The aim of this book is therefore to address this problem, and to look systematically at the reasons for writing a literature review, and how to go about doing it. Generally speaking, the longer the piece of work you are doing, then the more crucial becomes the review of literature. You will need to find and write about more examples of previous research, and the overall job becomes quite a major undertaking. This book will provide you with a step-by-step logical approach to the process, which should make it both easier and more interesting.

What then is a literature review? Well, when you are researching a topic, it usually has to be fairly narrow and focused, and because of this it can be difficult to appreciate how your research subject is connected to other related areas. The overall purpose of a literature review is to demonstrate this, and to help the reader to understand how your study fits into a broader context. For example, you might be carrying out an interview study of a small group of young people, to explore the difficulties they have in becoming established in a career. They will probably talk about a wide range of issues, many of which are personal or specific to them. However, when you come to write up your data as a dissertation, you will inevitably want to draw broader conclusions, and to apply your data to other related situations. You will also want to demonstrate that the question of finding a job or career for young people does not depend solely upon the young person themselves. There are wider factors in society which can affect their success or failure.

This is where the literature review becomes important. Whether or not a young person can find a suitable career definitely depends partly on the qualities and aptitudes of the individual person. However, it also depends upon the broad state of the economy; on government strategies to help young people into employment; on the current level of success of certain industries and sectors of employment, and on the availability of training and further and higher education. As part of your literature review you would survey what has been written and researched on these broad areas and their connection with careers and employment of young people. Having established the scope of existing research you would be able to show how your dissertation fits into the previous sequence of studies. You would be better able to make out a case that your study adds something to what is known about this matter. A literature review enables us to see how new studies and research are rather like building blocks, which are laid upon the ideas built by others.

A literature review therefore helps us to appreciate something of the sequence and growth of knowledge. As we survey the previous research on a subject, we may be able to identify areas which have not yet been investigated. These might suggest topics for future research projects, and also might suggest a particular focus or train of thought for our present dissertation. We thus can begin to think of knowledge as slowly accumulating in the past, and of research adding to this well into the future.

As you investigate what has been researched and previously written on a topic, you implicitly begin to justify the choice of subject for your own research. If a good many researchers have investigated different aspects of a particular topic in the past, then it is reasonable to assume it is an important topic. You might think, however, that there is a danger of repeating research, and hence making it very difficult to add to knowledge. This is not a problem which is likely to happen too often in the social sciences. For example, suppose that you are investigating the attitudes of a sample of 14-year-old school pupils to the issue of gender equality in society. You complete your interviews with the pupils, only to discover that a very similar piece of research was conducted two years ago in a school in a different part of the country. You are immediately worried that your research is not sufficiently original, and cannot possibly reveal anything new about the issue. Essentially, you need not worry.

The context of the first piece of research will have been very different. The school was different, and was located in a different catchment area in a different part of the country. The sample of pupils was certainly different. Besides the difference in the actual individuals, there may have been differences in the composition of the sample in terms of gender and ethnicity. The pupils will also have been taught by different teachers, and could be said to have had different educational experiences. We could go on listing such differences, but can sum this up by suggesting that there are so many different social variables between the two pieces of research, that there is little danger that the research will have been identical. In fact, sometimes this repetition of the theme of research is very useful in the social sciences, as it can reveal fresh nuances about a particular topic.

In a research study published in 2010, Shah, Dwyer and Modood examined some of the potential connections between educational achievement, social class and ethnicity. In the past there has been a good deal of research which has examined different contexts and permutations of the interaction between these variables. It is a contentious and problematic area, and no doubt there will be many further studies of various kinds which will examine the subject. It is an area in which there is a multiplicity of relevant literature, and yet the very complexity of the issues involved makes it relatively unlikely that any future studies could be seen as duplicating previous research.

Identifying the main subject and themes

By the time you start your literature review, you will probably have decided upon the main theme for your investigation, and also upon the key research objectives. To some extent therefore the essential task has been predetermined. You may have selected a research topic or theme around which a great deal of research has been previously conducted. If that is the case, it should not be difficult to find writing and research to review. In fact, the main difficulty may be in selecting what you want to include, and what you wish to exclude. However, if you have selected a fairly esoteric subject on which little has been written, then it may be difficult to find sufficient material to review. You may have to consider including a discussion of material which only exists on the periphery of the subject chosen.

There is every reason, therefore, when planning a research study or dissertation, that as many aspects of the research as possible are taken into account at the beginning.

Good practice

Research should not be treated as if it is a rigidly sequential process. In fact we often tend to present it like that in books, but it is not really an accurate picture. We can tend to think that we should select a research topic, then write the literature review, and then consider the kind of methodology to use. In fact, it is much more sensible to reflect upon all of these issues simultaneously during the planning and design phase of the research. Hence, before you finally decide on a research topic, it is best to conduct a quick survey of the available literature.

Are you happy with the range of literature which is available for this particular topic?

Does your chosen topic appear to fit in to a sequence of previous research studies?

In other words, decisions on research design are rarely taken in isolation, but should be seen as part of the overall research plan.

Suppose, for example, that you select the subject of business ethics for your research, and in particular wish to investigate the way in which products and raw materials are sourced from developing countries. It is difficult to decide on this subject with any certainty, without simultaneously taking into account the available literature and the way in which you intend to collect your data. For example, you might discover that there is relatively little literature on business ethics in relation to the specific countries you wish to use in your project. You would then need to decide whether that was a serious limitation on the research, or whether there was sufficient relevant literature in connection with other countries. In addition, you would need to consider the type of data you anticipated collecting, and whether this was realistic in relation to the countries you were intending focusing on in the study. For example, if you intended collecting data in the actual countries, have you sufficient resources to visit these countries? In short, then, research design should always be considered as an organic whole, and not as a series of separate stages.

Another important consideration in terms of the choice of subject is whether it can be subdivided into appropriate topic areas. The literature review chapter in a dissertation is usually one of the longest chapters, and it is usually helpful if it can be subdivided into sections, each representing a sub-theme of the research topic. Sometimes it is possible to make a connection between each of these sub-themes and the objectives of the research. In the previous example on business ethics, two of the research objectives could have been:

- to analyze theories of ethics which are relevant to the conduct of business in developing countries;
- to examine ethical aspects of the sourcing of food products from two West African countries.

When planning the research design for a subject such as this, it would be worth considering whether there was sufficient literature on ethical theory relevant to the study, and also on the ethical trade in food. If not, it would be necessary to consider how else the available literature might be subdivided.

Reviewing previous research

One of the basic aspects of a literature review is that there needs to be some selection process to decide which literature to include and which to exclude. When writing a research report, a journal article or a dissertation, there will normally be a limit in terms of the number of words. Decisions will need to be taken on which writers to include, and on the depth of analysis to be devoted to each.

However, it is very important to appreciate that a literature review is not simply a survey of one author or researcher after another.

Common pitfall

In early drafts of student assignments it is fairly common to see a literature review which consists of the mention of a series of writers, each with a few sentences devoted to them. In the worst cases, there may be no logical order to the presentation of the writers, and no apparent justification for their inclusion, other than that their work is broadly within the subject area. In cases such as this, the reader of the literature review is left to try to impose some sort of rational order on what has been written. If the reader is an examiner, then it might not put them in a very good mood!

Remember that in a literature review:

- There should be a clear structure.
- There should be an explanation for that structure.
- The literature should be presented in a planned order, for which there is a clear rationale.

When a series of literature is presented, along with a brief commentary summarizing the content of the research or article, then this is much closer to what is usually termed an annotated bibliography. This can be very useful to read, particularly if you need to survey a field very rapidly. It can provide you with a quick picture of the scope of a research topic, and what some of the main researchers and writers have said. However, it is typically a much more limited piece of work, without the depth of analysis and discussion which is associated with a literature review.

Although as we have said, a literature review does need a structure, and a number of different sub-headings and sections, it is essentially written in an essay style of writing. This is sometimes known as a discursive style. In other words, it is a style of writing which includes a number of different features including summarizing, description, analysis, discussion, evaluation, reflection and comparison. In order to achieve this style, a literature review cannot be brief, which explains why it is often the longest chapter in a student dissertation.

A good literature review will reflect the analytic abilities of the writer. When you are initially surveying the literature on a subject, try to look for trends, developments, contradictions or similarities which other writers might have missed or perhaps not discussed. It is often possible to identify places in the literature where writers disagree on an issue. It often surprises students that researchers and university lecturers sometimes differ on their interpretation of data or the conclusions which they draw from evidence. However, data does not always suggest a single, clear-cut conclusion, and this is particularly so in education and the social sciences where there are so many variables involved in research. If you can find instances where writers disagree on the interpretation of data, or where they take different approaches to an issue, this can often be very informative. It can, for example, shed light on the complexities of an academic issue, and help you explain that a question is not as straightforward as might be initially supposed.

Discussing previous research

Lever (2011), in a study of urban regeneration, contrasted two different views of government policy and strategy. On the one hand, he pointed out (p. 87) the perception of government as employing direct central control over the exercise and implementation of its policies. He then compared this model with a more recent practice of government allocating funds to partnerships which were expected to operate within fairly closely defined limits and parameters. Such semi-autonomous partnerships, while acting as an agent of government policy, did so with apparently more freedom of action. This contrasting of different models of government practice provided a framework within which the research could be analysed.

Emphasizing leading research studies

In any particular research area, some research studies will always be more influential than others. Some may be so influential that, in effect, they change the direction of a whole field of study. Research studies can become very influential for a variety of reasons:

- The research may develop and introduce new concepts which are widely applicable across the whole range of a field.
- These concepts may change the way we look at a subject area.
- They may therefore initiate many new avenues of research.
- They may result in the development of new methodological approaches.

When this happens, however, one of the almost inevitable results is that the research and the researcher become frequently mentioned in textbooks on the subject area, and are also widely cited by academic journal articles. So widely known is the research that you may indeed wonder whether it is worth mentioning it in your dissertation.

There is a matter of judgement here. If a particular study or theory has become in effect a classic or seminal work, and is widely taught at undergraduate level in a subject, then it may only need a passing mention in a research dissertation. Not to mention it at all, would probably seem like an omission, but on the other hand, it may seem trite to go into the details of a piece of research which is widely understood. It is very difficult to give precise rules here. In fact, making an appropriate selection from the available literature is part of the skill of writing a good dissertation. As you begin to learn more and more about a subject area, you will develop confidence in terms of understanding the nature of the research which is regarded as important and developing the nature of the subject. You will then be better able to make decisions about which literature to describe in detail and which to mention only briefly.

Indeed, one can argue that it is a key function of a literature review to define for the reader, the areas of work which are becoming important and which will have a profound influence on a subject in the future. The ability to do this comes gradually with a growing confidence in terms of one's understanding of a subject. In order to be able to recognize the influential research and key writers, it is important to search for literature in the relevant places. The researchers who are contributing to current developments in a field may well publish in the outlets which have the shortest publishing period. For example, edited books may have a fairly long period between initial concept and publication. Paper-based journals may be quicker, and electronic journals may be the quickest of all. Conference proceedings may be published some time after the actual date of a conference, and so may be of variable publishing time. If you can manage to attend them, then academic conferences provide the opportunity to hear about current developments, and also to engage researchers in discussion about their work.

One possible way in which you could structure your literature review in order to emphasize leading studies is to adopt a historical perspective. You could divide the literature into historical periods, ranging from the older classical studies, through more recent studies, to the latest research. This approach would enable you to justify discussion of older studies, while at the same time concentrating upon the more recent, developmental research.

It is worth mentioning, however, that what constitutes leading research in an area is, to a certain extent, a subjective, ideological question. Academics or researchers working in an area will place different priorities upon different facets of current research. One researcher may favour a particular methodology. In educational research, for example, some academics may prefer **quantitative** approaches to a research issue, while others may favour **qualitative** approaches using phenomenology or interactionism. In purely rational terms, the theoretical perspective adopted for a research study should relate to the nature of the research question. Some research issues, for example, are more susceptible to a survey approach in order to gain an idea of broad trends. Other research questions, particularly if they involve the investigation of human feelings or motives, may be better investigated by using qualitative approaches. When researchers work within a particular methodological framework on a regular basis, they can easily become very committed to that perspective. Hence they can favour those kinds of approaches, simply because they are working regularly within that perspective. Almost inevitably, if they are working regularly within a particular framework, they will tend to value more the latest research in that area, if only because they are more familiar with it. One can thus argue, that research, like other activities in life, has a number of different ideological perspectives, and individuals do tend to make choices, and to work within one framework rather than another. It may in fact be that research is not quite as objective as we often assume it to be.

Exploring key academic arguments

One of the interesting aspects of surveying the literature in a field is that it reveals the key concepts and ideas which form the basis for the study of that subject. Each distinctive area of a subject has its own range of concepts, which are used to express ideas in that subject. Some of these concepts may be shared with other academic areas, while some may be unique to the area in question. Understanding the concepts used to discuss and investigate a subject is central to having a full understanding of the subject.

When reading the literature of a subject, it is helpful to try to appreciate the nature of the concepts used. Some concepts such as 'motivation', 'feeling' or 'cognition' may be psychological in nature, while others such as 'socialization', 'community' or 'class' may be sociological. The former are concerned with the cognitive and thought processes of the individual person, while the latter are concerned with the place of the individual in society. Another range of concepts are those concerned with making value judgements. These are ethical or moral concepts, and are typically located in statements involving the words 'ought' or 'should'. If we say that 'this research should not be carried out unless we can guarantee the anonymity of respondents', then we are making a statement about research ethics. Some concepts may be concerned with the methodology of research. If there is considerable discussion in the literature about 'generalizability', 'sampling error' or 'empirical data', then we know that these concepts are concerned with issues of research methods.

Sometimes there will be a preponderance of certain types of concept within the literature of a subject area. Suppose we are surveying the literature on research in careers advice to young people. We might expect there to be a variety of concepts which are essentially psychological, since the career choices made by young people depend to some extent upon their personal psychological orientation. Some may prefer a practical job, for example, while others would prefer a job involving thinking and analysis skills. In order to give meaningful advice to young people we have to be able to interpret their psychological approach to the idea of a future job or career. When exploring the literature on this subject we would expect to identify concepts of this nature.

However, sound careers advice also involves explaining to young people something about the way in which a job is perceived in society. Young people need perhaps to appreciate that some jobs are held in higher status than others. Such jobs may have better conditions of service, and a range of peripheral advantages, such as the opportunity to travel. This higher status may also be reflected in better pay, both initially and in the long term. Young people may not have the understanding or experience to appreciate these factors, and good careers advice will generally point them out. In literature about careers advice, you would therefore expect to find some concepts which are fundamentally sociological or economic in character.

Having established the key concepts, it is much easier to appreciate the way in which academic arguments fit together. For example, if you have an understanding of the social factors which determine the context of a job or career, it is easier to predict the way in which a particular job might develop in the future. It might also be easier to predict the type of skills which could become more important. It is evident, for example, that there are likely to be increasing financial constraints on the staffing position in many jobs for the long-term future. Staffing costs are the single most expensive element in many areas of employment. This is likely to have consequences for the nature of a variety of careers. In teaching, for example, at all age levels, it is likely that there will be more emphasis on computer-based, autonomous learning in order to free teachers for other tasks. This may mean that the job of the teacher in the future may require sophisticated computing skills, and the ability to develop curriculum packages for self-tuition.

Economic considerations have probably also had an influence upon techniques for detecting and combating crime. Foucault has written extensively on the increased use of surveillance techniques in postmodern society, and indeed we appear to see the use of police surveillance cameras more and more. Changes in the nature of policing therefore seem likely to transform the traditional nature of the job of a police officer. The increasingly technical nature of many jobs means that we are moving more towards a knowledge-based society.

However, when you conduct an analysis of the literature in an area such as career developments, it is important to acknowledge that individual writers may approach the subject from different perspectives. One writer may be personally very much in favour of new technological developments, and may see technology as a means of improving the efficiency and effectiveness of a job. On the other hand, a different writer may be much more in favour of person-centred approaches at work. The perspective of a writer or researcher can have a significant effect upon the way in which they approach a research question, the way in which they write about it, and the type of concepts which they use in analyzing it.

Examining older literature in an area

What counts as 'older' literature in a subject area is to some extent a subjective matter. In addition, the question of age, in terms of literature, certainly depends very much on the subject area, and indeed the question of the length of time that subject has been recognized as a distinct discipline. The subject of computing has existed for such a short period of time, that literature published in the 1960s is likely to be considered of great antiquity! On the other hand, in, say, philosophy or theology, writing from one thousand years ago may not be considered particularly ancient! There are therefore judgements to be made about first of all what will count as older literature in a particular discipline, and, second, at what stage we may define a scholarly work as 'classical', and perhaps not requiring full explication in a dissertation.

The answer to these questions depends very much upon the nature of the research question, and how this has been formulated. A research question or the subject for a dissertation is usually expressed in a fairly precise and focused manner. For example, in the area of business education, you may be researching the performance of students on Master of Business Administration (MBA) courses. By definition, there is an immediate limitation on the literature to the period since MBAs were first offered in universities. If the research question were limited to MBA programmes in England alone, then this would place further limitations on the literature. In a research study of the development of nurse education in universities in the United Kingdom, there would be fairly precise parameters drawn around the selection of literature. This is a recent development, and although there may be some mention of earlier literature, the majority of that reviewed would probably date from the initiation of university-based education for nurses.

To take a very different example, we could consider the case of someone researching 'The ideas of Plato in a national curriculum'. There are fairly clearly two main areas of literature to consider here, the work of Plato, particularly in terms of **epistemology**, and then the nature of a centrally determined curriculum. In terms of Plato you would no doubt discuss some philosophical articles by contemporary scholars, but you would also need to analyze primary sources such as *The Republic*. In other words, there would definitely be a need to discuss older literature here.

In the field of comparative religion, there is also very often a need to discuss older primary literature. In a study of 'Hindu ethics in contemporary Indian life', it would again be necessary to analyze two principal types of literature. You would need to decide on a number of ethical issues which were significant for various reasons in contemporary India, and then locate relevant literature. Second, however, you would need to analyze these in terms of Hindu teachings on morality and ethics. In order to do this systematically, it would be necessary to discuss the parts of Hindu scriptures, such as the *Bhagavad Gita*, which address ethics. You would also, of course, discuss writings where academics discuss Hindu ethical principles, but it would also be better to examine the original scriptures.

Developing a historical perspective in the research

In any area of study, there will almost certainly have been a development and evolution of ideas. This 'history of ideas' may on some occasions have reflected parallel changes in society at large, or in other cases may have itself influenced society. In entire disciplines such as sociology, we can look back at the changes that have occurred. During its initial phase of development, with writers such as Comte and Durkheim, sociology was oriented very much towards quantitative approaches to measuring society. There was the assumption that society could be analyzed and measured in much the same way as physical phenomena could be investigated. Society was assumed to consist of a series of facts or **variables** which were related to each other in terms of scientific laws. The job of the sociologist was to uncover these laws.

As the study of the discipline continued, however, sociologists started to think of society in much more fluid terms. They began to view it less in terms of fixed laws, and more as something which was continually changing. They began to see it as a product of the interaction of human beings. Within this view, society is not seen as a fixed, objective entity, but as something which is continually constructed and reconstructed by human beings. To a certain extent, with some variations, this perspective has continued to this day.

The same kind of evolution of ideas has also occurred within narrower, more focused subject areas. As you survey the literature, and get to know the field better, you will be able to discern these kinds of historical trends. It is also worth noting that in many subject areas, academic work has been conducted in a variety of countries, not simply within the English-speaking world. One of the decisions you may need to take is whether, or to what extent, to discuss literature in other languages.

Portraying the literature on a subject in a historical sequence is a simple, and often attractive option. However, although presenting material in chronological order is one of the most basic and popular ways of structuring data, it does have a potential disadvantage. As the literature is presented in date order, from one section to another, there may not be any particular connection between one section of the literature and the next. The only connection is the chronological sequence. There may not be any connection in terms of themes, subject matter or trends. The ideal situation is where a historical sequence of the literature corresponds with a sequence of ideas, but this may simply not be the case. A simple historical sequence may be useful, but if a choice has to be made, then a thematic sequence of the development of ideas should reveal far more about the particular subject, and indeed the underlying development of concepts and knowledge within that area.

Summarizing new and developing knowledge in an area

One of the commonest fears of students is that just after they have handed in their dissertation for assessment, there will be some major development or study in their area of research! Even worse is the anxiety that the examiners for the dissertation will know about that research, and will ask them questions on it in the oral examination! Well, it is simply not possible to be absolutely up to date in a subject, and the examiners will realize that. However, a good literature review should present and analyze the latest research as far as is reasonably possible. In order to do this, you will need to search sources of literature such as conference proceedings, which present the latest research. During your research you may even be able to develop contacts with professional researchers, who will give you pre-published summaries of the work they are doing.

It is also important to bear in mind, as mentioned in the previous section, that there may be relevant sources of research available in languages other than English. The significance of this depends very much upon the subject area which you are researching. Where a topic is intimately connected with another country, then there will almost certainly be material being published in that country. In the area of Religious Studies, for example, if you were researching some aspect of the Sikh religion, then it would be sensible to survey publications from India, and particularly the Punjab. Some journal articles would be in English but others would be in Punjabi. The extent to which you could access these would depend upon your linguistic abilities or obtaining translations.

Some academics from non-English-speaking countries have had a major influence upon thinking in different disciplines. In France, for example, we could point to Pierre Bourdieu and Michel Foucault in educational studies, and Jean Baudrillard in cultural studies. Foucault has also been influential in other areas such as criminology. The principal books of these writers have been translated into English and are widely available, but there remain many journal articles and conference papers, published in French, which would only be available to those able to translate from the original. Although it is easy to assume that English is almost becoming the lingua franca of academic study throughout the world, it is very important to remember the enormous amount of scholarly literature which is published all the time in other languages. For most types of research study you may not be expected to analyze literature in other languages, as it might arguably be unfair on the part of the examiners to expect you to be bilingual, but it would at least be possible to indicate in your literature review that such a body of research existed. It might also be possible using your school French, German or Spanish to survey some of the academic journals in other languages, in order to indicate where articles on a topic were being published. If you could do this, it would show an awareness of the scope of publication in an area.

In terms of identifying the most recent research in an area, it may also be that in some topics research in the country of origin of a particular thinker or issue may be more up to date than in English-speaking countries. In the country of origin, researchers will have access to all kinds of contextual material and data which will be unavailable in other countries. They will also be able to make links and connections with other writers from that country. Imagine, for example, a research student in, say, Norway or Italy, writing a dissertation on Shakespeare, and using only sources published in their own country and language. We would find this rather strange to say the least! In a globalized academic world, we need increasingly to take a very broad view in terms of identifying key literature on a subject.

It is also worth noting that the latest research in some areas is publicized in populist media sources. Researchers in areas such as clinical research or education, will sometimes disseminate their provisional findings in newspaper or magazine articles, or on the radio, in order to raise awareness of their work. This often helps in attracting a larger audience for the research, and perhaps even, in some types of research, to attract additional funding. From the point of view of the student, it can be very useful in drawing attention to the latest research, and subsequently enabling you to seek out more formal articles written by the researcher or research team.

Writing about a new and developing area

There can be both advantages, and at the same time, distinct difficulties, about analyzing a new area of research. Hedenus (2011), for example, decided to investigate the lives of lottery winners. She decided to examine the manner in which they conducted their lives after their winning. The advantage of a new topic is that it is likely to be a relatively under-researched area, and therefore offers new opportunities. On the other hand, with new topics it is not always easy to identify research samples when there is not a great deal of existing previous research to act as a model.

Identifying gaps in our understanding of a subject

We cannot know everything about a subject, and almost inevitably there will be gaps in our knowledge. These gaps in understanding may be due to a variety of factors. Within a particular subject area:

- Some issues may appear less interesting to researchers.
- Some topics may attract less public attention.
- Some research questions may not have attracted research funding in the past.
- It may be more difficult to collect data on some issues.

In a perfect world, it may be desirable first to identify an apparent gap in the research literature, and then to develop your research proposal in that area. However, it is not necessary to think that research should always be on a subject within a gap in the literature. Valuable research can be done in terms of investigating a well-researched area. It is often extremely useful to obtain results which apparently confirm previous findings, or in fact, which do not confirm previous findings. Karl Popper's Theory of **Falsification** argues that scientific enquiry should primarily be concerned with seeking empirical evidence which falsifies previous findings. He argued that this was more methodologically rigorous than always looking for data to support a theory.

Nevertheless, one of the useful outcomes of a literature search should be to identify apparent gaps in previous research. The existence of a gap in the literature should at the very least cause us to try to find an explanation for this, and such an enquiry may result in a more sophisticated understanding of the subject matter.

In some subject areas research may be largely non-commercial; that is, there will be no immediately evident possibilities for income generation from the research. In many areas of educational research this is the case. In areas such as this, the possibility of income generation is not a key factor in deciding which area will attract the most research studies. However, in other disciplines, particularly in technology, engineering and the applied sciences, there will be many potential economic advantages for some types of research. Potential industrial and commercial applications will generally lead to research sponsorship of various kinds or of the possibility of patentable products. The possibility of income generation may be a major factor in determining that one area or issue is extensively researched, while another issue attracts relatively little attention.

Exploring trends in the literature

One of the functions of a literature review is to identify the broad developments or trends in the way literature on a subject is developing. However, the way in which this is achieved, and the particular trends which are identified, depend to some considerable extent upon the focus of the review. For example, a literature review might focus primarily upon methodological developments in a subject, or it might tend to concentrate upon the way in which social and political changes have affected research on a subject. In some cases, one might argue that methodological trends are linked to social changes.

In educational research there has sometimes been a tendency to concentrate on quantitative measures. Attempts have been made to relate social class to educational performance. Various models have been developed in order to measure social class, and to relate these to quantitative measures of student performance. Quantitative research has tended to be popular with social planners and politicians, who are seeking to understand broad trends in society, in order to make large scale economic decisions about educational policy. Quantitative research has also tended to be employed when people want to measure trends in performance across the country, or even to compare educational performance in different countries. Qualitative methods, on the other hand, have tended to be used when it was necessary to understand something of the detailed lives of people, and how they interacted with each other.

One of the ways in which trends can be discussed in the literature, is to examine first of all the publications which tend to address the broad issues in a subject area, and then to analyze the literature which concerns the more specific topics of your research subject. In other words, there is a progressive focusing from the general issues to the those more narrowly related to the subject. It is generally easier to locate literature on the broader themes of a topic since it is possible to cast a net fairly wide in the search for suitable material. As you focus more and more narrowly towards your specific dissertation subject, you may find some difficulty in locating literature. This may be that you are being too demanding on yourself, in trying to find literature which is closely related to a very specific subject. You may have chosen such a precise, narrow subject for your dissertation that very little research has been done on it before. If that is the case, then you will probably need to broaden the scope slightly, of the kind of the literature you are seeking.

An example of moving gradually from a general topic, to focusing on a more specific one, occurs in a research article by van de Werfhorst and Luijkx (2010) on the subject of social background and education. The article starts by noting generally 'that inequality of educational opportunity is prevalent in many western and non-western societies' (p. 695). The article then proceeds to a more specific concept of 'effectively maintained inequality' (p. 696).

Summarizing key ideas in a subject area

Determining what you consider to be the main trends in the literature you have analyzed is related to the question of the key ideas in the subject. The decision as to the main trends almost inevitably involves a decision about the key research studies and hence the key ideas in a subject area. The nature of some of the key ideas will be determined because they are in effect the seminal ideas, probably associated with internationally known researchers and writers. However, the other ideas which you choose to highlight will to some extent reflect your own subjective position on the research articles which you have located. You may be influenced by the author of the article, whom you perhaps know has written several other influential articles. You might also be aware that some writers have been cited in other articles you have read, which gives them a certain credibility. You may have eliminated the conclusions and ideas from some articles, because you feel there are methodological failings in the research. On the other hand, you may have included some articles because you feel that there is the potential for future research based on them, or that their ideas are potentially influential within a broader perspective.

Overall, the selection of the key ideas from a body of literature is a very important function of a literature review, and reflects the analytic process undertaken by the researcher. This selection process also inter-relates with the attempt to define an original contribution to knowledge from within the research dissertation. Part of the concept of a contribution to knowledge is that the latter interlinks with the key areas of knowledge as previously defined.

When you are writing the conclusion to your research and making out the case for the contribution to knowledge made by the dissertation, it is good practice to refer back to the literature review. In this way, you link together the different elements of the dissertation, and help to create a piece of writing which is a coherent whole.

Key terms

Epistemology: the study of the grounds upon which we believe something to be true.
Falsification: the assertion (often associated with the philosopher Karl Popper), that it is logically more rigorous to gather data in order to attempt to negate a theory, than to support it.
Qualitative data: data which is in the form of words, e.g. interview transcripts or historical documents.
Quantitative data: data which is in numerical form, e.g. questionnaire responses or measurements.
Variable: in research, a quantity which varies in nature or magnitude.

Key questions

1 If you have already chosen your research subject, and yet cannot find very much specific literature on it, what strategies could you use?
2 If you want some of the literature you use to be very recent, what would be the best kind of literature to use?

3 In what ways would you try to link a literature review with other parts of the dissertation, in order to ensure that the dissertation was a coherent whole?

Key reading

Aveyard, H. (2010) *Doing a Literature Review in Health and Social Care: A Practical Guide*, 2nd edn. Maidenhead: Open University Press.

Hart, C. (1998) *Doing a Literature Review: Releasing the Social Science Research Imagination*. London: Sage.

Jesson, J., Matheson, L. and Lacey, F.M. (2011) *Doing your Literature Review: Traditional and Systematic Techniques*. London: Sage.

Machi, L.A. and McEvoy, B.T. (2009) *The Literature Review: Six Steps to Success*. Thousand Oaks, CA: Corwin Press.

Ridley, D. (2008) *The Literature Review: A Step-by-step Guide for Students*. London: Sage.

2

The content of a literature review

*Summary • Learning outcomes • The categories of literature to include
• Defining the range of the review • Selecting areas related to the subject
of the dissertation or research study • Credibility of journals • Relating
the content of your review to the research aims • Areas of contention
• Key terms • Key questions • Key reading*

Summary

Having explored the purpose of a literature review, this chapter examines the
nature of the literature to be included in such a review. Of all the different
categories of literature which could be included, this chapter discusses the
way in which we can choose the most appropriate types. It analyses the ways
in which we can relate the type of literature to the subject matter of the study,
and also how we can evaluate the types of academic journal to use.

Learning outcomes

After reading this chapter you should be able to do the following:

- Know the different types of academic literature which could be included in
  a literature review.

- Understand how to select appropriate academic journals from which to choose articles.
- Relate your choice of literature to the subject of your study or dissertation.

The categories of literature to include

There are a number of different ways of categorizing the literature to be included in a review. One of the most basic is to compare literature which includes primary research data within it; another is to consider literature which discusses a topic and includes references to other studies.

In the first category, the author or authors of the literature are usually the researchers who collected and analysed the data which is discussed. Most scholarly journal articles come into this category. Some journal articles report on small-scale research studies which might perhaps have been carried out by a university lecturer, or by a professional practitioner such as a teacher or social worker. In such a case, in effect all of the research study is reported within a single journal article. In other cases, a journal article may only report on part of a larger research study. Sometimes a team of researchers in a university, or even a consortium of universities will bid for and obtain a research grant to fund a large study. Such research might be a **longitudinal study** which will last a number of years. As part of the programme the research team might employ a number of postgraduate students who will assist with the research and write up different parts of it. They might use some of the data for their own doctorates, and may also write journal articles in consultation with academic staff. Each article would typically only report on the particular aspect of the research project being conducted by the student. Normally authors should make it clear when an article is reporting on a piece of self-standing research, or, when it is reporting on an element of a larger study.

Most scholarly journal articles have a fairly standard structure and layout. They start with an abstract which provides a summary of the whole article. There is then an introduction to the context of the research, and a brief literature review. Typically this is followed by a discussion of the research design and methodology. The data is then analysed and discussed, and the conclusions presented. A list of references ends the article, although there is also usually a note of contact details for at least one of the authors of the article. You will find a wide range of such academic articles in the list of references at the end of this book.

When researchers in any subject area conduct research, they usually report it through the medium of the academic journal article. This is accepted as the standard way of reporting research within the academic community. It serves the purpose of disseminating research to those who are interested in the subject area, but also of enabling other academics to read and check the methods used to draw conclusions. When work is placed in the public domain in this way, researchers across the world can gain from the research done by others, and also challenge work which they feel could have been conducted in a better way. It is because of the checks and balances associated with this way of reporting research, that many feel that the academic journal article should be one of the main types of study analysed in a literature review.

There are many other types of journal article which are published, notably those in so-called **'professional journals'**. Most professions such as teaching, accountancy, management, social work, nursing, and so on, have their own journals, often linked to professional associations, which publish articles of interest to those working in that area. Most articles are concerned with issues of professional practice, and designed to further and enhance practice in that profession. The articles included are typically much shorter than academic articles, do not have the same degree of referencing, and are generally written in a less formal style. The professional journals may also include photographs and other illustrations which are not normally found in scholarly journals. Professional journal articles may include some primary data, but it would normally be on a limited scale. It would be wrong to say that such articles should not be included in an academic literature review, because for some subjects they may be relevant. However, it would normally be better to concentrate on scholarly articles, particularly in a postgraduate dissertation.

Another type of publication which normally concentrates on discussing original research is the chapter in an edited book. An academic, or perhaps several authors, will develop an idea for a book in a particular field and then ask a number of scholars active in that field to each contribute a chapter to the book. In this way a number of different contributions in a field are assembled to provide different perspectives on a particular subject. Each chapter is, in many ways, similar to an academic journal article. Such books have the advantage that a theme within a subject area can be explored from a number of different points of view. The disadvantage of the edited book, however, is that the time from inception of the idea to publication may be rather longer than the publication time for an academic article. This is particularly so with the rapid increase in the number of electronic journals, which typically have a shorter publication time than print-based journals.

Sometimes research is also reported in booklets or books which are termed monographs. These are more substantial accounts of primary research than are usually given in academic journals. Publication of such longer accounts of a fairly narrow research subject may be justified because, for example, the subject may be of topical significance. Some publishers specialize in such publications, although there are usually not many copies printed since the market is likely to be restricted. When postgraduate students finish their doctoral thesis, they are sometimes able to secure its publication in monograph form. As most doctoral theses are very specialized, they do not necessarily attract a great deal of interest when published. However, some may do so, because of their contemporary relevance. Monographs of all forms, including published theses, are very relevant for inclusion in an academic literature review. In addition, unpublished Masters and doctoral theses are often discussed in scholarly literature reviews.

In a strictly research-oriented literature review, it is probably the norm to concentrate on literature which contains primary data, usually collected and analysed by the author. However, other types of literature should not necessarily be rejected, simply because they are not focused exclusively on newly collected data. The vast majority of academic books which are published are not monographs or devoted to primary data. They are basically concerned with presenting existing knowledge, very often in a novel way, or from a new perspective. They are often loosely described as 'textbooks', although I would argue that this term does not really do them justice. It tends to imply that the book simply contains a systematic summary of existing knowledge, as if the way in which that knowledge were presented was unproblematic. Yet, knowledge is seldom uncontentious. What counts as valid knowledge in a particular area, is often the subject of discussion and argument. An author will often explore these debates and nuances of interpretation, and in so doing, add something to our understanding of the subject. This may not be the case with all books, but certainly it applies to a good many. Hence, textbooks should not be automatically rejected as potential material for literature reviews.

Common pitfall

There are a good many popular textbooks on research methodology which are widely read in higher education. Students often cite these in their dissertations at all levels, including at doctoral level. Tutors and examiners will often accept these works in undergraduate dissertations, but will be critical of them at Masters level. They would probably regard them as unacceptable at doctoral level. There is then in a sense, a kind of hierarchy of acceptance of such works! It is very difficult sometimes for students to distinguish which books would be acceptable at different levels; and it has also to be said, that opinion varies also between academic staff. It is very difficult, if not impossible, to provide specific advice. However, in general terms, if a book provides straightforward description of methodological approaches, then it is probably suitable for undergraduate level. If it provides analysis and discussion of those approaches, pointing out advantages and disadvantages, and comparing different approaches, then it would probably be more suitable for Masters level. Finally, if it sets those approaches within the context of actual research studies, as reported in research articles, and discusses their effectiveness, then such a book might be appropriate at doctoral level. If you are unsure about the suitability of a particular book, it is best to discuss the issue with your tutor or supervisor.

Articles and accounts on the internet can pose particular problems in terms of a literature review. By these I do not mean scholarly articles published in e-journals, but the more general kind of documents and articles which proliferate on the internet. Sometimes, if a subject area is of minority interest, and little research has been conducted on it, the available academic literature will be sparse. In such a case, students may be very tempted to use more populist articles from the internet. Whether these are appropriate or not depends very much upon the context.

On one occasion some of my students were researching various aspects of new religious movements. The latter were often very small organizations, some of which had achieved notoriety through extreme, and sometimes violent behaviour. In some cases, the scholarly literature had become quite voluminous, usually because of the large-scale publicity attracted by the organization. However, in other cases, there was very little formal literature, but a wide variety of informal documents. Many of the latter were to be found on the website of the organization, and might be overtly proselytizing or certainly biased in favour of the organization. The problem with using such documents in a literature review was to ensure that the degree of bias was evaluated and discussed. Such articles could not be presented in the same way as scholarly articles. In short, internet articles may be used in a literature review, but should be carefully appraised and analysed in order to assess the degree of their objectivity and neutrality.

It is also worth briefly evaluating newspaper articles for inclusion in a literature review. Generally speaking, only articles from newspapers with a high level of journalistic and literary content should be used. In addition, it is worth bearing in mind that newspaper articles may be more relevant to some research subject areas than to others. One can imagine that they might be very useful for research studies in fields such as politics, public administration, social policy, international studies and media studies. In other areas such as technical aspects of science and technology, they would not be able to treat the subject with sufficient mathematical or scientific detail. However, in an area such as public attitudes towards energy generation, then newspaper articles might be very useful.

Finally, it is important with newspaper articles to evaluate the perspective from which they are written. Much more than is the case with journal articles, newspaper articles may display a degree of ideological bias. This does not necessarily affect their usefulness, but it is important for you to discuss and analyze their particular approach.

Defining the range of the review

One of the most basic aspects of writing a literature review (or any other chapter of a dissertation for that matter) is to decide on the anticipated length.

You need to make an estimate of the length of the projected chapter in both words, and in typed pages. In order to achieve this, you need to know the overall required length of the dissertation, and the number and names of the chapters which you intend to include. Some chapters will inevitably be longer than others. You therefore need to have an approximate idea of what will be included in each chapter. It should then be possible to estimate which chapters will be the most important in the final dissertation, and hence which will be longer and which shorter. It is often a good idea to allocate an estimated word length to each individual chapter.

The first half of most dissertations consists of an introductory chapter, a literature review chapter followed by a chapter which discusses aspects of research design, methodology and theoretical considerations. The second half of the dissertation consists of several chapters in which the primary data is presented and analysed. In the first half of the dissertation the literature review chapter is normally the longest of the three chapters. The methodology chapter is the next longest, and finally the introduction is the shortest. If anything, the first 'half' of the dissertation will often be slightly shorter than the second half. Therefore, in a dissertation of 80,000 words, the first half might be 35,000 words in length. The relative lengths of the chapters might be 16,000 words for the literature review, 11,000 words for the methodology, and 8,000 words for the introduction. These figures are only approximations, and you might very well alter them considerably depending upon the nature of the research subject. A chapter of 16,000 words is quite long, and you might decide to divide it into two separate chapters. Alternatively, a judicious use of sub-headings could divide up the material, and give the chapter a structure which is easier for the reader.

At any rate, you now have the approximate chapter length, and can use this to calculate the approximate number of references and citations required. If we assume about 250 words per typed page, then the literature review chapter would be about 64 pages long in the actual dissertation. We can now estimate the number of references you will need to find.

It is very important in a literature review chapter that quotations from texts do not become so predominant that they monopolize the chapter, and overshadow what you write yourself. The essence of the chapter should be your analysis, illustrated and exemplified by quotations. Very long quotations of half a page or more, can be tedious to read, and contain too much material for the reader to absorb. It may be better to restrict indented quotations to about four or five lines. This would mean that you could have about two quotations per page, giving a total number of quotations needed for the chapter of 128. Assuming that each quotation will come from a separate book or article, then this will require 128 publications.

These 128 publications are the ones which you will discuss in the literature review. However, you will almost certainly also wish to cite a wide range of publications. By this I mean that after having discussed a topic or subject, at the end of the last sentence of the discussion you might include in brackets the names of several authors and relevant years of publication. The purpose of this is to indicate the names of writers and academics who could be consulted for further information on the topic. Academics often include quite a number of such citations in journal articles. They add substantially to the scholarly credentials of what you have written. In a chapter of 64 pages it would be quite reasonable to add 150 such **citations**. In total then, you would need just short of 300 references for your chapter! This may seem a little daunting, but at least it is better to have an estimate of what you will need, rather than leaving everything to chance.

Having made an estimate of the total number of references needed for the literature review, the next step is to apportion these between the different sections of the review. In other words, you would need to decide on the different themes of your review, and then allocate a proportion of your total number of references to each section. The selection of themes for your review depends very much on the overall subject of the research.

We have spent some considerable time discussing the length of the literature review, since this is fundamental to determining the range or scope of what is included. There may be all kinds of criteria and factors which determine which works should be included and which excluded, but probably the most significant factor will be space. If you do not have the room to include a discussion of something in the chapter, then it simply cannot be included. This is why it is very important to undertake the planning exercise as above, in order that you have the best possible idea of the space available.

Good practice

Although we can talk about the general principles of structuring a dissertation, it is important to remember that writing a dissertation is ultimately a creative activity. One of the best ways of gaining ideas of how to structure a literature review, and also of how to create a sense of balance between the literature review and the remainder of the dissertation, is to look at examples of previous dissertations. When you do this you at least have the reassurance that these dissertations have been 'successful', and that therefore their structure and layout have been accepted by the examiners.

When you look at dissertations in a library, or in an electronic archive, you will undoubtedly find some variety in the way they are presented. The literature review may be divided into two separate chapters, and indeed may not be termed a literature review in the chapter heading. An examination of previous dissertations will give you a sense of the extent to which you can reasonably vary your structure, without moving too far from accepted norms.

Selecting areas related to the subject of the dissertation or research study

There are various ways in which the sub-divisions of the literature review can be related to the dissertation topic. In a research dissertation it is quite common that the researcher selects a perspective or paradigm to use for the analysis of the data. Such a perspective might be methodological in nature. In other words, the overall approach of the dissertation may owe a great deal to, say, an interpretive perspective or a phenomenological perspective. In this case the data collection strategy for the research would be typical of those methods used in **interpretivism** or phenomenology. Equally, when the data is analysed, then the fundamental concepts of these two perspectives would constitute a framework for the data analysis. Where the approach is basically methodological, some of the discussion and analysis of the approach may take place in the methodology chapter, and some in the literature review chapter. The extent and nature of this division may depend on the inclination and judgement of the writer.

The literature review section may examine the work of the early writers in each field, for example, Weber and German idealism in the case of the interpretive approach, and Husserl in the case of phenomenology. Having examined the early contributors to the field, you may then consider the literature from more contemporary writers who have used one or other of the perspectives. If there were to be some discussion in the methodology chapter, then this might concentrate on practical issues concerning data collection and analysis.

The establishment of a theoretical perspective in research can be very useful indeed. Importantly, it gives an intellectual focus to the research. Without it, the research will consist of some data being collected, followed by the analysis. This may be quite satisfactory for some types of research, but there will be nothing to set the research and conclusions within a broader scholarly context. There will be very little to connect the results with the conceptual frameworks of other research studies. However, a theoretical perspective provides a conceptual framework not only for the analysis of the data, but also within which the conclusions can be connected with previous and future studies.

There are other ways in which a theoretical perspective may be generated for use within a research study. One of the most popular is to select the work of a leading researcher or academic, which can be used to analyze a range of data. Normally a relatively well-known academic is selected, and usually one whose theories or ideas can be applied in a relatively wide range of contexts. An example of someone whose ideas have been widely used in academic studies is Karl Marx. Many researchers have used his ideas of political economy and of social class to interpret a diverse variety of data. A writer who has been widely used in this type of approach is the French sociologist Bourdieu. In a recent study, Erel (2010) used Bourdieu's ideas to analyze the situation of Turkish and Kurdish women who had migrated to Britain or Germany. Erel was interested in the way in which the knowledge and skills of the women (conceived as a form of 'capital'), derived perhaps from their personal qualities or achievements, or perhaps from their ethnic background, could be used to help them become successfully established in their new country.

In the article, there is first a general introduction followed by a discussion of research on the subject of Turkish and Kurdish migration to Germany and the UK. This is followed by an analysis of the concepts of human capital and ethnic capital, and then of Bourdieu's notion of capital. Finally, these ideas are used to analyze the case studies of individual migrants who have settled in the UK or Germany.

When following this type of approach it is important to select a writer whose ideas can be easily applied to the subject of your research. It also helps a great deal if you can find several other studies which have employed the same concepts in their analysis. The reason for this is that it is important to be able to establish the relevance of a theoretical approach. After all, if we wanted we could pick any theoretical approach, but it might not have any relevance or suitability for our research. For your dissertation to have a sense of coherence, it is important that the examiner can see that the perspective used links with the research subject and the data. It helps in making this case, if you can point to previous uses of the perspective.

A major advantage of using a well-known figure such as Marx or Bourdieu is that there will usually exist a substantial body of literature which discusses both the thinker personally, and also analyses their work. It is therefore relatively easy to have a major section of the literature review which discusses the theoretical perspective and its originator. Other sections of the literature review can then concentrate on significant aspects of the research subject.

Narrowing or broadening the topic

In terms of the structural elements of the literature review, when you are writing your dissertation, you will be concerned with making sure the review is sufficiently long and detailed; ensuring it discusses the relevant aspects of the subject area; and trying to make certain that the review interrelates with other parts of the dissertation.

With regard to the first point, one of the issues is that you need to write a sufficient quantity to establish that your dissertation possesses the qualities of doctoral work. It is not easy to achieve this if you curtail the length of the literature review, or any other section of the dissertation for that matter. The overall dissertation may seem not to have sufficient substance for a doctoral study. Of course, making it clear that you are writing at doctoral level does not depend solely upon the length of your dissertation. There are many other factors. However, managing to achieve approximately the correct word length is an important factor. On some occasions you may find that the subject matter has been so well researched, that you will exceed the overall word length. Your job will then be to reduce the word length appropriately. If, however, the word length is not sufficient, then you will need to find fresh material to analyze and to discuss. When looking for extra material, it is often necessary to be flexible in terms of the topics which are covered. You may need to stray into subject areas for the literature review which are not very closely related to the central subject of the dissertation.

It can be helpful to think of the possible subjects for a literature review as a series of concentric circles. The central circle represents the principal subject of the dissertation, and the next circle a slightly less-relevant subject. As we move outwards from the centre, each subsequent circle represents a slightly more peripheral topic. The harder it is to find relevant literature, then the more you will need to move outwards to the peripheral circles. It is generally much easier to reduce the length of a literature review than it is to find more material. You can use a variety of criteria to reduce the length. You might decide, for example, that you prefer to use journal articles and to dispense with some of the book references, or perhaps to have more subject-based references and fewer devoted to methodological issues. However, expanding the literature review, by looking for new subject areas, poses more complex problems.

An interesting way to analyze the scope of a literature review is to use the key concepts employed in a research article, and to relate these to the list of references at the end of the article. Many academic articles list a series of 'key words' at the beginning of an article, to provide an indication, along with the abstract, of the subject matter of the article. By comparing these key words with the list of references, it is possible to judge the emphasis which the writer placed upon certain topics in terms of using literature. It might also provide evidence of which topics provided the most useful source of potential material.

Broadening the literature review

As an example of this approach we might take the research article by Freytes Frey and Cross (2011). This article is entitled 'Overcoming poor youth stigmatization and invisibility through art: a participatory action research experience in Greater Buenos Aires'. It is possible to consider each key word mentioned at the beginning of the article, and then to count the number of references which appear to relate to a particular key word. However, it should be noted that the key words are not necessarily an exact analytic tool. It is not always easy to allocate citations to a particular key word with any certainty. However, this method does give an approximate guide as to the spread of literature used in the review. The following is the list of the key words, with the approximate number of citations related to a particular key word:

Arts (6), Local Emergent Knowledge (2), Participatory **Action Research** (3), School Abandonment (4), and Subaltern Populations (6). There are also four citations of the work of Bourdieu, who is used to provide a theoretical orientation to part of the research.

Most research, and indeed research articles, is specialized to different degrees, and this can make it difficult to identify a relevant body of literature to analyze. This article appears to be an example of this. The list of references is not very long, compared to many articles, and this may have been because of the specialized nature of the subject. In addition, the citations are apportioned fairly equally between the different key words, suggesting that there was no single key word which provided a large body of literature. This type of analysis therefore provides us with an idea of how authors can draw upon a broad range of topics for the review, and also of the way in which students may need to be fairly eclectic in their choice of literature.

Credibility of journals

One of the methods used by the readers of research to judge the quality of a literature review is to evaluate the journals which have published the articles in the review. Arguably the most important characteristic of academic journals is that articles accepted for submission will have been '**peer reviewed**'. This process entails several stages. An article which has been submitted to the journal, comes first to the journal editor, who reads it to decide whether the article is broadly suitable for the journal. The editor may take into account general issues such as the relevance of the subject matter to the mission statement of the journal; the extent to which the article complies with the submission guidelines; and whether or not the article is presented in accordance with accepted academic conventions of style and referencing.

If the editor is satisfied that there are no major or overwhelming reasons for immediately rejecting the article, then it will be sent for review to two academics. The author's name and institution will be removed from the article, before sending it for review. Some journals have an editorial board of fixed membership, from whom two members are selected to receive the article. Some journals have a perhaps smaller editorial board, and a larger informal network of academics who are willing to review articles. In the latter case, an article may be reviewed by the extended network of scholars, and then perhaps by one or two members of the editorial board. The article author does not know the names of the reviewers, nor are the latter published at all in the journal. One reviewer does not know the identity of the other reviewer.

The journal usually produces a proforma for reviewers to complete, which has a list of criteria by which the article should be judged. These might include such issues as the range of literature reviewed, writing style, precision and relevance of aims, selection of methodology, explanation of data analysis, discussion of ethical issues, and accuracy of referencing style. Generally speaking, the reviewers may recommend acceptance of the article without amendment; acceptance with minor amendments; referral with a suggestion that the article be resubmitted with major amendments, and outright rejection. The reviewers usually read and comment on the articles 'blind'. That is, they read the articles independently, and are unaware of the views of the other referee. The editor will probably hope that the reviewers form broadly the same judgement of an article. This enables the editor fairly easily to summarize the views, and reach a decision to transmit to the author. Where the views of the reviewers are very different, the policy of journals may differ. The editor may send the article out to a third reviewer, or he or she may arbitrate themselves. In some cases, the editor may have help from a deputy editor in resolving such problems.

In general, the rigour of this process is one of the most important marks of the quality of the journal. Another important yardstick is the amount of time taken by the process. It is usually important that research is published relatively quickly once the data has been collected and analysed. Ideally it needs to reach the attention of other researchers while it is still topical. For this to happen, the reviewers need to read and comment upon the article promptly. As the reviewers are normally working academics, lecturers and researchers, they are not always able to respond very quickly because of the pressure of other work. However, electronic submission and transmission of new articles, coupled with on-line commenting by reviewers, has tended to speed up the process. Many journals now publish the reviewing 'history' of an article, noting the date when it was first received, and then the date when the revised version was received. The reviewing interval is typically between three months and six months.

The role of the editorial board

Another important aspect of quality for a journal is the nature of the editorial board and its members. Most academic journals are very specialized. They tend to publish articles on a narrow subject, and gradually develop a reputation in that area. Academics who teach and research in that area will normally know the main journals which are relevant to them, and will either subscribe themselves or ensure that their institutional library does so. They will often submit their own articles to this range of journals, and will know personally or at least be familiar with the names of other authors who publish articles in these journals. Academics will usually wish to publish their articles in what they perceive as the most prestigious journals in their area. Sometimes a journal will organize an academic conference under its auspices, at which academics in the field of the journal can meet, present conference research papers, and discuss the latest developments in the area. Such conferences also add, by association, a certain prestige to the journal.

The editor and the composition of the editorial board are one of the key factors determining the status of the journal. The editor is usually a leading academic in the field, often a professor at a prestigious university. The editorial board also usually consists of leading academics, who have published widely in the particular field. Generally speaking, if these academics are highly regarded, then this enhances the status of the journal.

Some journals are sponsored by or connected with a professional academic association. So, for example, the *European Journal of Teacher Education* is connected to the Association for Teacher Education in Europe. This kind of academic link helps to enhance the prestige of both the Association and of the journal. They each benefit from locating themselves within a community of professionals and academics with the same interests. It is also worth mentioning that in the contemporary globalized world, linked by electronic versions of journals, academic publishing is truly international. Journal articles need to address an international audience, and journals need to be aware of their wide readership. It is important that the composition of editorial boards reflects this international role, and draws upon members from a wide range of countries and institutions.

The role of academic journals is a complex and important one. Many of the factors discussed above have an effect upon the reputation of an academic journal. Although it would be very difficult to formally rank academic journals, nevertheless many of these criteria do have a bearing upon the informal status and credibility with which academic journals are regarded. When selecting articles for a literature review, you will probably, and quite rightly, be guided principally by the content of the article and its relevance to your dissertation. Nevertheless, it is best to be aware of the credibility of the journals you use, and the potential of the more celebrated journals to add something to your literature review.

Relating the content of your review to the research aims

The aims of an academic dissertation are the key factors which determine the rest of the thesis. They are statements of intent which set out the goals of the research. The way in which they are expressed has logical consequences for the data collection method, and the strategies for analyzing the data. Supposing that an aim is, for example, to survey the age of appointment of a sample of school head teachers or principals, then this implies that quantitative data will be collected, probably using a questionnaire. It further suggests that the data may be analyzed statistically.

On the other hand, if a research aim involved the analysis of social interaction between care staff and elderly people in a residential home, then this would imply an interpretive or qualitative approach to the collection of data. It would also suggest that the data analysis might involve an interpretive process such as the use of grounded theory. In addition, when the research has been completed and you have clarified your findings, it is normal in the dissertation to review the aims in the concluding chapter. It is here that you evaluate the extent to which the aims have been achieved. If they have not been adequately achieved, then it is usual to discuss the limitations within the research which have prevented the full achievement of the aims.

The importance of the aims within a research dissertation is that they have an integrative function. They link all the different elements of the dissertation together, and give it a sense of cohesion. When it is being read, there is a sense of direction. The aims act like signposts in the dissertation, and help the reader to anticipate what will come next. When you are writing the dissertation, you can keep referring back to the aims, so that the reader maintains a feeling for the purpose of the research.

This is particularly important in the literature review. It is important for the coherence of the dissertation that there is a clear justification for the different sections of the review. The aims can provide this clear justification. Indeed, each aim could generate a particular sub-section of the review, and this would again help the reader in understanding the structure of the dissertation. An academic dissertation is a very complex document, and if the writer is not careful, the reader can easily become confused and fail to find any line of logic within the general argument. As you write the dissertation, if you keep referring back to the aims, and to the related sections of the literature review, then everything which you subsequently write will have a clear context. The reader will be able to see how any single part of the dissertation is connected to all other parts, and that everything can easily be traced back to the literature review.

Areas of contention

In terms of the content of a literature review, there are a number of areas and issues which may cause an examiner to question what you have written. These areas include:

1 The use of very ancient literature, even though the works may be regarded as classics.
2 Citing internet pages without evaluating their quality.
3 Summarizing works sequentially, with a small amount of discussion, but without relating the literature to each other.
4 Using unpublished sources without analyzing the degree to which they can be considered objective.

A research literature review is fundamentally what it says. It is a review of previous research on a subject, subdivided into a number of categories. The notion of scientific research as we know it, is usually associated with the dissemination of scientific rationalism, and its gradual popular adoption as a means of thinking about the world. We might date this approximately from the mid-nineteenth century onwards. From roughly that period, there has been an exponential growth in empirical research, until it has now become a major world-wide activity. Although ancient sources have contributed a great deal to many disciplines, it has usually been in the area of conceptual clarification, and the analysis of theoretical ideas. Generally speaking, the sources discussed in a modern literature review will need to be works which reflect the contemporary empirical research tradition.

The internet has made an enormous contribution to this tradition. It has made it possible to disseminate research findings extremely rapidly, and to make it possible for academics and researchers to utilize the findings of research very quickly. In a related development it has encouraged the growth of open-access journals, and the much freer availability of knowledge. It has also enabled researchers in different parts of the world to communicate with each other much more easily, and hence to collaborate more effectively. A negative aspect of the internet, however, has been the ability of people to disseminate their views, subject to little or no editorial control. The result has been that the consumer of the internet has needed to exert their own judgement and editorial control, where normally in the case of books or paper-based journals, this would be exercised by publishers. In terms of literature reviews, the internet has thus to be used with great caution, and the items selected for discussion should be subjected to very careful analysis, particularly with respect to subjective or biased opinion.

It is important to remember that the overall philosophy of a literature review is more sophisticated than merely listing books and journals with a brief discussion on each. A literature review should be a very creative activity, which attempts to inter-relate the literature on a subject in new and novel ways. If it limits itself to being simply a list of works with brief comment, then it will not be well regarded by the examiner.

Finally, the use of unpublished material can be a contentious issue. This is not to say that unpublished material has no academic quality. In fact one has only to think of research dissertations themselves, which are often very valuable sources of data and previous research. Many academics write articles and discussion papers which they do not necessarily seek to publish, but simply make available to friends and colleagues in order to stimulate discussion. Then there are letters, emails, and other responses to enquiries which can be cited as 'unpublished' if they are made available to you. It would be wise, however, and certainly courteous, to seek the permission of the author before including such material in a dissertation.

Key terms

Action research: a research perspective which seeks to use collaborative methods in resolving practical, everyday research questions; often those which occur in the work place.
Citation: the mentioning of a scholarly work in a piece of academic writing.
Interpretivism: a research perspective which is the opposite of positivism. It seeks to understand the way in which human beings construct their own social world.
Longitudinal study: a research study which investigates changes in variables over an extended period of time.
Peer reviewing: the submission of a piece of scholarly writing to other academics to gain their views.
Professional journal: a journal which concentrates on providing discussion of contemporary, vocationally-focused issues relating to a particular professional area.

Key questions

1 How would you select a writer or academic to use as a source of a theoretical perspective for your research?
2 What would you list as the main functions of the editor of an academic journal?
3 What criteria would you use to select newspaper articles which were suitable inclusion in a dissertation literature review?

Key reading

Cooper, H.M. (1998) *Synthesizing Research: A Guide for Literature Reviews*, 3rd edn. London: Sage.

Feak, C.B. and Swales, J.M. (2009) *Telling a Research Story: Writing a Literature Review*. Ann Arbor, MI: University of Michigan Press.

Fink, A.G. (2010) *Conducting Research Literature Reviews: From the Internet to Paper*, 3rd edn. London: Sage.

Galvan, J.L. (2009) *Writing Literature Reviews: A Guide for Students of the Social and Behavioral Sciences*, 4th edn. Glendale, CA: Pyrczak Publishing.

Hart, C. (2001) *Doing a Literature Search: A Comprehensive Guide for the Social Sciences*. London: Sage.

3

Doing a literature search

Summary

This chapter examines the different strategies which can be used to identify the literature to be discussed in the survey. Increasingly the methods used involve electronic searches. However, there are still decisions to be taken about the criteria for the search, and exactly how it will be conducted. The chapter will also investigate the use of non-traditional sources of literature, and the ways in which these can be accessed.

Learning outcomes

After reading this chapter you should be able to do the following:

- Conduct a search of literature suitable for a research review.
- Evaluate different electronic databases for their relevance to an academic research review.
- Analyze different sources of literature according to their relevance for a research literature review.

Preliminary survey

There are a number of different ways in which the initial decisions about a literature search can be taken. Much depends upon the research subject and the way in which this subject was chosen. For example, it is not uncommon for students to select their research subject based upon the known existence of an extensive source of literature. When I was a student, one of my tutors told me about a large archive of overseas newspapers which could be used to support several different research topics. The idea was that I could study the archive with a view to generating a research question for which there was ample supporting data and literature. In another example, I was informed about a little-known archive of correspondence and documents relating to one of the major ballet companies of the early twentieth century. Again, it was suggested that this could form the basis of an interesting research thesis.

We normally assume that the process of conducting a literature search develops from an initial decision to select a research topic. However, if we select a research topic without any prior appreciation of the extent of the available literature, then we may leave ourselves with a lot of work in identifying areas to search. Even if we identify areas to search, we may find very little relevant literature. It is therefore at least worth considering to do things the other way round. If you can identify a body of research literature, and then work backwards to a suitable research topic and aims, then you may save yourself a good deal of effort. It has to be admitted that this approach may not appeal to the purist researcher, and it certainly is not the completely logical way to proceed. However, as we have discussed on several occasions before, research is not always the logical, linear process that we would sometimes like it to be. We sometimes have to be prepared to move sideways, backwards and diagonally in our thinking and planning, and not just forwards!

It is sometimes advisable with certain specialist subject areas to carry out a preliminary survey of the literature, before deciding firmly on a research subject. One possible strategy is to identify several journal articles in the area in which you are interested, and then study the list of references at the end of each article. This will give you a quick introduction to the literature of the field. Some of the references will probably be specific to the article, but there will be others which are either seminal works in the area, or more general works of wider applicability. You will probably find that at least some of the more general works are cited in different articles. In this way, you will begin to survey the field of relevant literature for your subject. You can then search for other articles by the same authors, and some by authors mentioned in the lists of references. This is a rapid way of beginning to understand the background literature of your field. It is not a particularly systematic way of going about the task, but if time is at a premium, it is one worth considering. Having gained a fairly rapid idea of the nature of the background literature, you should begin to construct an understanding of the types of research topics which have been investigated. This should give you some ideas of how research in this area could be progressed, and how new topics could be identified.

Another variant on this method of a rapid search is to start with an article by someone working in a particular field, and then find her or his CV on a university web site. Journal articles usually name the institutions in which the authors research or teach, and most universities maintain accessible databases of their staff, with lists of their research interests and publications. The CVs may also list the conferences people have attended and the papers they have delivered. There may also be available some full print copies of other articles they have written. In this way, you should be able to identify not only the range of scholarly work of an individual, but also the names of other academics with whom they work, through, for example, the identification of joint-authored publications.

Determine the key words in the subject area

The identification of the key words of a research study is the first essential step in identifying the relevant literature. Unless this is done in a careful, logical way, you will probably fail to identify some of the key areas of literature. To take a hypothetical example, we might consider a research dissertation entitled 'Social interaction in the multicultural classroom'. This research project could have the following possible aims:

• To analyze the role of religion in the multicultural classroom.
• To explore the significance of mother-tongue communication in multicultural education.
• To examine the factors which affect the integration of children in a multicultural environment.

From the title and aims, we can fairly easily identify some key terms. These might be:

• Interaction
• Multicultural classroom
• Religion
• Mother-tongue
• Communication
• Multicultural education
• Integration
• Multicultural environment

Preparing a summary of key terms

Having extracted an approximate list of terms from the research title and aims, you need to reformulate the list so that similar terms are grouped together. The above list could then become:

- Multicultural classroom
- Multicultural education
- Multicultural environment

- Interaction
- Integration

- Communication
- Mother-tongue

- Religion

The next step is to think of concepts which are related to each of the above four groups. The first group could include Multiculturalism, Ethnicity, Culture, Classroom environment, Classroom culture, Race, Multiracial education, Ethnocentrism, Eurocentrism.

The second group could include Symbolic interactionism, Participation, Citizenship, Unity, Collaboration, Society and Representation.

The third group could include Language, Linguistics, Socio-linguistics, Psycho-linguistics, Conversation, Discourse, Grammar and Pronunciation.

The fourth group could include Faith, Belief System, World View, Theology, Divinity, Prayer, Ritual, Ceremony, Worship and Scripture.

The final step is then to conduct searches using different search engines and databases, using the concepts from the title and aims, and the related list of concepts. This should then start to generate academic literature, and other source materials.

One of the most precise approaches to searching for terms and concepts is to use **Boolean logic**. This enables you to open up a search to a larger number of potential sources or to narrow it to only those sources which connect a specified number of concepts. In order to widen a search, you can use the conjunction 'or'. Therefore if you searched for 'multiculturalism' or 'ethnicity', then it would locate sources which mentioned only multiculturalism, or only ethnicity, or both concepts. A series of concepts could thus be linked together, to create a very broad search.

On the other hand, if you searched for 'citizenship' and 'society', this search would only retrieve those sources which mentioned both citizenship and society in the same article or reference. The conjunction 'and' thus narrows a search considerably. Sometimes you may wish to search for a key idea, but related concepts keep intruding into your search, and widening it unnecessarily. In this case you can use the instruction 'not'. Hence, if you wanted to search for references including the concept 'ethnocentrism' you might find that a lot of sources referring simply to ethnicity kept intruding on your search. Therefore you could search for 'ethnocentrism' not 'ethnicity'.

In a more complicated search, involving several different concepts, you can employ brackets to define your search more precisely. The contents of brackets are typically dealt with first by a search engine. Thus if you searched for 'scripture' not ('ceremony' or 'worship'), this would first of all locate anything which included the concepts ceremony or worship, and then remove those from any sources which mentioned 'scripture'. This would then make your search for sources on scripture much more precise. You might use a search for this in a situation where you were researching the subject of scripture in religion, but did not want to concern yourself with situations where scripture was used in relation to ceremony or worship.

If you want to make a very broad initial search for a group of related concepts, then you can use the symbol * after a word. For example, if you search for 'socio*' you will obtain references for every term which begins with 'socio' – a great many references indeed! These will include such terms as sociology, socio-cognitive, socioeconomics, socio-legal, socio-demographic, and socio-cultural, to mention only a few.

The age of the literature

When you are writing a literature review it is important to be as up-to-date as possible with your sources. Clearly, when you are writing a dissertation, the work has to end at a particular moment in time. You submit the dissertation on one day, and all those important research articles which are published the next day are inevitably not included in your dissertation! Nevertheless, there is a viewpoint that although your written review must end at a particular moment, the reviewing process continues. If you have an oral examination (or viva voce) for your dissertation, then there are advantages in continuing to monitor publications throughout the intervening period between submission and examination. Your examiners will be subject-specialists, and will be familiar with the current literature on the subject. They may even have written a good deal of it! It is therefore very wise to be as current as possible in your understanding of the literature, even after the submission of your dissertation.

A knowledge of the most recent literature in your subject area is very important. However, in recent years there has been an enormous expansion in academic research publishing, particularly in terms of the proliferation of academic journals, and the very large number of articles which are submitted to each journal. The number of research articles published by an academic is one of the major criteria used to judge their performance in their job, and this is one of the key factors influencing the number of articles produced. The worldwide expansion of higher education has also been another factor in the increase in the number of articles being written.

However, this expansion has also led to considerable time delays in the publishing of articles. The peer-review process can be time-consuming, and even when an article has been accepted by the editor of a journal, there may still be a waiting period until there is space in the journal to publish the article. This situation has led many academics to make their papers and articles available to the broader academic community, either in advance of submission to a journal, or at the same time it is submitted. They may place their article on their own institutional website, or as part of their CV. There are also databases which specialize in the archiving of 'pre-published articles', often known as 'pre-prints' or sometimes simply as 'e-prints'. One of the best known is an open access site maintained by Cornell University Library and known as arXiv (Cornell University 2011). This site tends to specialize in scientific disciplines and in quantitative finance and statistics. The advantage of **pre-publishing** is that it enables the academic community to continually familiarize itself with the latest thinking and developments in a field, without being handicapped by the time-delays of the peer-review system. Whether or not you decide to include pre-prints within your literature review, an awareness of the latest ideas will certainly be a potential advantage in the dissertation viva examination.

The recency of references is an important factor in judging the quality of any academic writing, whether a literature review in a dissertation, or a journal article. When you are selecting articles for your review, you should certainly at least, check on the relative recency of the references used. Indeed, some scholarly journals make the recency of references a factor in deciding whether to pass on a submitted article to the peer review stage of the acceptance process. This is true, for example, of the *Leadership and Organization Development Journal* (Emerald Group 2011).

One form of literature which is likely to be up-to-date is the conference paper. Academics and researchers attend academic conferences in order to present their latest research to the academic community, to discuss their current research which is in progress, and to hear about the work of their colleagues. Many conferences publish the papers which have been delivered as 'Conference Proceedings'. Some conferences are also sponsored by or associated with academic journals, and after the conference a selection of papers is often published in the journal.

The normal pattern for having a paper accepted at a conference starts with the submission of an abstract of the proposed paper, between six to nine months before the conference date. The conference committee then selects the abstracts which seem most relevant to the conference, or perhaps those which seem most likely to generate interesting papers. The authors are then asked to submit the full paper perhaps between three to five months before the conference. The papers will then typically be submitted for peer review, often by two reviewers acting independently. On the basis of this process, papers will be accepted for the conference. It will often by the case, as with journal articles, that authors will be asked to make different degrees of amendments to their papers before the final submission. It is evident from this sequence of events that conference papers are, first of all, valid scholarly publications because of the review process, and, second, that they are normally relatively up-to-date. Hence if you are either able to attend conferences, or obtain a copy of a presented paper, then you can feel fairly confident of its currency. After the conference, the papers will be collated as 'proceedings' and usually deposited electronically in an index such as Thomson Reuters ISI Index to Social Sciences and Humanities Proceedings (Thomson Reuters 2011a). From there they can be accessed by the worldwide academic community.

University repositories

University **repositories** are a normally open-access database of the research and publications output of an institution. The authors are usually the academic staff, researchers and students of the university. The repository movement has expanded very rapidly in recent years, facilitated by the ease with which documents, articles and theses can be archived electronically. Repositories provide an easily accessed and searchable source of articles and other research output. You can access a university repository via the university web site, or by using one of a number of directories and organizations which list repositories on a worldwide basis. One of the best known is the Directory of Open Access Repositories (OpenDOAR) (University of Nottingham 2010). Other organizations which support the open-access repository movement include the Registry of Open Access Repositories (ROAR) (University of Southampton 2011), and the Scholarly Publication and Academic Resources Coalition (SPARC 2011) which is based in Washington, DC. ROAR provides up-to-date information on university repositories around the world, while SPARC is a network of academic libraries, and is dedicated to examining new strategies for making academic research widely available.

The repository movement is very much linked to the concept of the open availability and dissemination of research output, for the benefit of the academic community in general. Besides research, different institutions place other kinds of information in their repositories, including a range of institutional data and discussion papers, which might be of general interest. Archived material in repositories may include theses and dissertations, e-portfolios, academic articles, reports of research in progress and book chapters. A repository enhances the image of an institution by providing a window through the means of which a university can publicize the work of its staff and researchers. In addition, it provides a management tool whereby institutional managers can monitor the quality and range of the research output. As the research output is usually uploaded directly by the author, then there is every likelihood that it will have been written fairly recently and, from the viewpoint of age, will be sufficiently recent for your literature review.

The variety of material which may be saved in a repository will include:

- Experimental records
- Data sets
- Statistical records
- Monographs
- Books
- Chapters in books
- Journal articles
- Theses
- Diaries
- Autobiographical accounts
- Family history archives
- Institutional history archives
- Local history collections
- Patents
- Musical compositions
- Audio recordings
- Video recordings
- Conference proceedings
- Output of research societies or centres
- Specialized collections
- Proceedings of learned societies

Grey literature

There is a great deal of literature output which is not generated by publishers in the form of journals, magazines or books. Broadly speaking, all the literature which is produced which is not part of the mainstream, published market, may be categorized as **grey literature**. The following are just some of the different categories of grey literature, and this is definitely not an exhaustive list!

Types of grey literature

- Reports of various kinds. This may include business and company reports; reports on various technical and scientific matters; and internal organizational reports on the viability of projects.

- Newsletters, magazines for internal organizational consumption, brochures, circulars, zines, internal organizational literature, and official publications of various kinds.
- Working papers, discussion documents, plans for projects, proposal forms, and summaries of new initiatives.
- Agendas, minutes of meetings, conference papers, conference proceedings, conference posters, and fact sheets.
- Course materials, lecture notes, transcripts of talks, interview transcripts, PowerPoint presentation slides, copies of emails, and diaries.
- Dissertations, theses, research notes, essays, student assignments, questionnaires, data collection instruments, and translations of texts.

There are several online databases which attempt to classify and make available a large quantity of grey literature. The System for Information on Grey Literature in Europe (OpenSIGLE 2011) enables you to carry out searches for grey literature, while the Grey Literature Network Service (GreyNet International 2011) encourages analysis and research on grey literature.

In terms of research, grey literature has both advantages and disadvantages. Much of it is produced very quickly, and so is very directly connected with the thought processes of the person who has produced it. The writing may have a directness and immediacy which is to a certain extent lost in conventional literature. Since it may not have been subjected to a prolonged editing process, it may more closely represent the feelings of the writer. It may therefore be very useful for autobiographical or life history research. In this context we might think of diaries or transcripts of talks. In ethnographic research, where the purpose is to construct an account of social interaction and its context, many of the items of grey literature listed above might be useful as either data or for the literature review. This would depend upon the context of the ethnographic research.

There are, however, lots of potential difficulties with the use of grey literature in literature reviews. The documents may be undated, and the author of the documents may be unclear. Equally, the organization or individual who has physically produced the documents may be uncertain. All of this may make it rather problematic to cite the document in an orthodox way. As the origins of the document may not be known, it can be difficult to discern the reasons for producing it, and hence to appreciate the ideological content of the document. Equally it may be difficult to validate and verify the content of the document. All of these factors may make you hesitate before using grey literature in a literature review. However, it could be argued that it is better to take each case on its merits. If the particular document appears to shed some light on the research question, and to be connected with the history or content of the research, then it may be reasonable to include it. However, it would be wise with all grey literature to make sure you discuss its potential drawbacks and limitations at the time you cite it. This shows that you are aware of these potential difficulties, and appreciate that it is necessary to be circumspect with this type of document.

Wikis, blogs and RSS

The opportunities for electronic communication are expanding at an exponential rate. This affects all sectors of society, and academics have been as quick as most to realize the potential for their work. The increased access to knowledge and ideas has particularly affected research, and extended opportunities for research students to search for data and published research. Indeed, as the extent of research activity increases, and more and more research outputs are being made available, research students have to cope with an ever expanding volume of research to investigate for their thesis. This, in itself, poses new problems. Although we have more and more electronic tools to enable us to keep in touch with other researchers, and to track their research findings, this is also creating previously unanticipated issues. One of these issues is that as more and more people become involved in research activity of various kinds, it is not easy for research students to be able to evaluate the quality of what they are reading. It is also not easy for you to assess whether the content of electronic sources is appropriate to include in a literature review.

Blogs are a popular form of communication, enabling people to express themselves on issues, add their opinions to a debate, comment on the views of others, ask questions, and to exchange information and ideas. Universities often support blogs in different subject areas, via their virtual learning environments, to enable students to exchange ideas. Academics also often contribute postings to further the discussions. However, the difficult question is the extent to which you can feel that you can use such material in your dissertation and literature review.

Postings do vary enormously of course, in terms of length, detail, academic rigour and quality, and research content. Some may be brief, superficial comments, while others may be very carefully considered evaluations of an issue. Some comments may be posted by undergraduates, some by postdoctoral researchers and some by professors. The sheer range and variation encountered on blogs make it rather difficult to decide whether something could legitimately be included in a dissertation.

Much depends of course on the subject of a research project. If, for example, you were conducting research on new forms of electronic learning and their viability and popularity, then it would be very likely that you would use examples of blogs as part of your data. You may also employ extracts from blogs in your literature review, depending probably on the academic status of the person who made the posting, and on the level of analysis and discussion in the blog. It should be said here that in this field of the use of new forms of electronic communication in research dissertations, we are in a rapidly changing area. The norms and conventions of research dissertations do not remain constant. They are forever evolving, and doctoral examiners reflect the changes in the ways research is taught in universities. As universities incorporate more and more different types of electronic communication between students, between staff and students, and between academic staff themselves, these innovations will affect not only teaching styles, but approaches to assessment as well. It is difficult to pre-judge the ways in which this will affect research dissertations and the types of material which are considered to be legitimate. There is a growing body of research on electronic learning styles, and as such dissertations start to employ a diversity of different electronic sources to discuss and evaluate, it seems likely that this will affect research studies in other subjects.

If you want to use different types of electronic material in your literature review, and are unsure about the degree to which it would be accepted, then there are two main strategies you could adopt. The first is to consult your supervisors, and take their advice. The most important factor in deciding whether to use a particular form of electronic literature in a literature review, is whether you have an adequate justification for its use. You should try to think out clearly the reasons for wanting to include a particular document or piece of text, and discuss these reasons with your supervisor. If you feel the justifications are adequate, then you need to articulate these in the dissertation for the sake of the external examiners. The other justification strategy is to try to find successful previous dissertations which have included the kind of electronic literature which you are proposing to use. You can then cite these dissertations as evidence that this type of approach has been considered legitimate previously.

Many of the issues discussed above with regard to blogs also apply to the use of **wikis** within academic communities. Wikis are increasingly being used to enable students and researchers to work together on shared problems and questions, and to collaborate in terms of knowledge, research strategies, research literature and the design of projects. They enable communities of researchers to contribute to hyperlinked web pages, and to share ideas and expertise. There are issues about the editorial control of wikis to ensure the validity of the material, and this is a factor which should be taken into account before using such documents in a dissertation. There have traditionally been concerns within academic circles about the use of documents such as wikis, which enable multiple users to add content to a web page. However, as with most forms of electronic multimedia, practice in the academic world is changing very rapidly. Wikis are now being used to encourage students to work together on the same project, and lecturers are able to identify the elements added to the wiki by each student. This enables wikis to be used as part of an assessment system.

The rapid expansion in the availability of research information is an enormous asset, but at the same time it is very difficult for research students to find the time to keep up to date with the increased output of articles, conference papers and books. This problem has led to the creation of various electronic mechanisms for sending people automatic messages when there is a new publication or development in their area of interest. Such current awareness services are a valuable means of saving time, as you do not need to keep visiting websites separately time and time again, just to check whether there has been a new publication or whether a new conference is being planned. At the same time, there may be many websites of which you are generally aware, but do not have the time to explore thoroughly. By setting up an alerting system, you can ensure that you receive news of new developments on websites which you may not have explored extensively.

There are a wide range of publications and organizations which provide different kinds of current alerting systems, and enable you to track new events and output. Academic journals normally will alert you to their table of contents for new issues, so that you can check whether an article of interest has been published. Conference organizers often have awareness mechanisms to let you know about the titles of papers which are to be delivered, or indeed to alert you to conferences which are planned in the future. Publishers also will inform you of new books in your research area, and any other developments which may be of interest.

One of the commonest systems for keeping up to date with developments is the use of **RSS** (Rich Site Summary) feeds. To receive these you need a RSS feed reader such as Bloglines® (2011). The number of feeds is expanding rapidly, and you can select the particular subject areas in which you are interested. Major research sites such as that of the European Commission (2011) have a large number of feeds to which you can subscribe. Despite the volume of material available through these alerting mechanisms, it is important to keep one issue in mind.

Common pitfall

It is perhaps wise to always remember that the ultimate purpose of searching for the very latest information is the production of an academic dissertation or a journal article. The literature search is not an end in itself! You do not receive your research degree, or get your article published on the basis of a sophisticated literature search, although that will no doubt help a good deal. With this enormous expansion in the access to information electronically, it is easy to be swept away into devoting far too much time to this. You will not gain any specific credit for the number of electronic literature searches that you carry out; for the number of potential citations which you find; for the number of possible quotations that you save in your database; or the variety of different databases which you consult. The sheer range of information available makes it seem very attractive to keep carrying out more and more searches. However, it is not necessarily profitable to acquire far more possible citations than you really need. That will only make the selection process more complex.

When your dissertation is finally evaluated, the quality of the literature review will be considered in the light of the citations included, not those which have been excluded! It will be determined by the level of analysis, the way complex ideas are integrated with the rest of the dissertation, and the way in which the relevant literature is sub-divided and then synthesized. When you are conducting your literature searches it would be best to remain focused at all times on the final goal or target of these searches. Remember what you are trying to produce, and do not get too drawn into the actual search process.

Using referencing and bibliographic software

As you are conducting your literature search, you will probably find that one of the major issues is managing and organizing the considerable amount of information which you will accumulate. The crucial information to record are the details of the book or article, in order that you can compile your list of references at the end of your dissertation or essay. If you think you might want to include a quotation from a book or chapter, then you will also need to select the quotation, and type it into your records, along with the page number of the book. It is generally much better to do all this recording of information at the time you read the book, so that you have it ready when you are actually writing the dissertation. It is so easy to read a book, and think how useful it would be in the dissertation, and then to return it to the library, full of intentions to borrow it again when you are writing up your research. You may then find that you have either forgotten the author, or that someone else has borrowed the book!

When you are reading a book for the first time, it is often the case that you will spot interesting quotations for your dissertation. However, besides recording the actual extract and page number, it is worthwhile also making notes on the reason for selection, and the way in which that extract fits into the rest of the book from which it came. If you do not note down this information you may well find that when you begin to write your literature review, you have forgotten the reasons for selecting the quotation. It may just seem like an isolated passage, and you will not be able to link it into the remainder of your argument. The only recourse will be to retrieve the original book from the library, and re-read the relevant section to get a sense of the argument and discussion. This will be time-consuming and frustrating.

So great is the quantity of information you will accumulate, that you will ideally need a carefully planned data management system to handle it. It is also desirable that as you begin to read and amass information, that you develop an on-going classification system which reflects the way in which you will structure the writing of your literature review. As argued earlier, it is in some ways a good idea to relate this structure to the aims of the dissertation, so that the literature review is linked to other parts of the dissertation. Whatever structure you decide upon, you will need to accumulate your new references and additional notes in some kind of data storage system which works for you.

Probably the simplest storage system to use is to open a series of Word files for each section of your literature review, and to record references and quotations in those files. Although this may seem a little laborious, it does have one or two advantages. You control the input of information, and the accuracy and consistency of the reference presentation are entirely within your control. If you take care doing this, then you can feel confident that the finished product will be accurate. In addition, when you are recording unusual source material such as grey literature, you can adapt your system of recording as you feel necessary. There is therefore a sense of control over the entire process. On the other hand, research students and academics are increasingly using one of the referencing and bibliographic software packages to manage their data. There are a variety of these commercially available, although one of the most popular is EndNote® (Thomson Reuters 2011b).

EndNote enables you to search internet databases for references and source materials, and to import these to your collections of citations in EndNote. These collections of references are usually termed 'libraries' in EndNote. You can also add references manually to your lists. When you are writing your literature review you can add citations to your text from EndNote. In addition, you can select the type of format, such as the Harvard System, in which you prefer your references to be printed. Within the different lists of references, it is possible to sort the data in a wide range of different ways, in order to help you find material in the future. It is also possible to add comments and notes to these lists to remind you of relevant additional information. However, as with most software packages, there are various protocols for entering data, and it is necessary, for example, to use the correct punctuation when entering references if these are later to appear in the form you wish.

> ### Good practice
>
> The advent of more and more specialized computer packages in the field of social science research has brought immeasurable advantages. However, there are also one or two issues of which one should be aware. An example is the use of statistical analysis packages, which have taken so much of the laborious calculation out of quantitative data analysis. However, occasionally students treat such packages as if they can wave a magic wand to analyze their data! The data, however, will only be analyzed properly if the correct statistical procedure is selected, and if the data is entered in the package in the correct way. Finally, the emerging results need to be interpreted correctly. All of this requires a knowledge and understanding of statistics. In other words, although these packages save an enormous amount of time in terms of carrying out lengthy calculations, they do not remove the necessity to possess a sound understanding of statistical procedure. It is a similar situation with spell checkers on computers. Although very useful in highlighting errors, one cannot assume that they will automatically correct all of them.
>
> The same principle applies to the use of software packages when carrying out literature searches and managing bibliographical information. The best approach is to regard such packages as removing a great deal of the labour from the process, but remembering that you should still check the output at all times, to ensure the form and content is as you would want it.

Library catalogues

Most students looking for materials will normally start with the library of their own institution. With the ease of on-line searching, this can then be extended to other academic library catalogues. There also exist various consortia of libraries and catalogues which are very useful for identifying source materials. The Copac® National, Academic and Specialist Library Catalogue (Copac® 2010) provides free access to the combined catalogues of a variety of institutions, including universities, specialist libraries and national collections. Members include the library of Trinity College Dublin, the British Library, the Victoria and Albert Museum, the National Portrait Gallery, and the National Libraries of Scotland and Wales. All of the institutions which are members of Copac® are listed on the website. The combined catalogue has in the region of 36 million entries. When you locate a document in which you are interested, it may be possible to gain access to it through the inter-library loans system.

Copac® remains a catalogue, and not a database or collection of articles and books. Although it may be possible in some cases to gain access to full-text materials by following internet links, normally Copac® lists the titles and other relevant details of a publication, and notes also the source of that publication. You will normally need to use other methods to find a copy of the publication. There are also materials available in a variety of languages. Copac® is based at and administered from the University of Manchester.

If you wish to actually use other academic libraries, then you can register via your own institutional library with SCONUL (2009), the Society of College, National and University Libraries. You will be issued with a card which will enable you to access other libraries. Members of SCONUL include all the university libraries of the UK and Ireland.

Another example of an integrated library catalogue is WorldCat®. This enables you to have access to a very large number of major academic libraries, including those of the University of Washington, the University of California, Berkeley, Cornell University and McGill University. Like Copac®, WorldCat is basically a very large integrated catalogue, which enables you to identify the location of academic materials. In some cases, you may be able to obtain full-text versions, through electronic links. Typically, however, you will need to make enquiries at a library to which you have access or borrowing rights. You can also access WorldCat via your mobile phone, by inserting the url www.worldcat.org/m/ into your browser. The British Library (2011a) is also a valuable source of reference material for researchers. It is a legal deposit library, and holds approximately 14 million books, nearly one million journals and newspapers, and three million audio recordings. The British Library Integrated Catalogue may be searched free of charge.

Dissertations are an extremely valuable source of information for research students, and can often be included in literature reviews. One of their most valuable uses is that they enable you to scrutinize a dissertation which has 'passed' – which has been accepted as being of the correct standard. You gain an idea of the way in which a dissertation is structured, and the way in which the data is presented. You begin to appreciate the balance between the chapters, and the way in which the writer combines new data and results with information from previous research studies. Formerly, successful dissertations were archived in university libraries as hard-bound paper copies. If you wanted to read a dissertation produced and archived at a different university to the one at which you were studying, then you had to borrow a copy through the inter-library loan system, and then consult it in your own library. The advent of electronic storage has considerably streamlined this system.

Initially, dissertations are stored electronically in the university repository at which the degree was awarded. They are usually also then stored electronically on EthOS-Beta, the Electronic Theses Online Service (British Library 2011b). Not only does this database store recently produced dissertations, which were produced electronically from the beginning, but EthOS is also in the process of arranging the scanning and storage of dissertations which were produced before the digital age. The system currently has over a quarter of a million dissertations for consultation, and in order to expand this, universities are being encouraged to require their research students to submit dissertations electronically. The system has revolutionized the availability of research dissertations, since students can now consult the full text of the dissertation at a considerable distance from the library at which it is stored. Previously, only one person at a time could study the dissertation, but now many people can read the dissertation simultaneously. It also means that expensive shelf space in libraries can be used for other materials.

There is one aspect, however, to the electronic storage and open access to research dissertations which has given rise to some potential concern. Research students often like to publish all or part of their dissertations. Sometimes this takes place in the form of journal articles prior to the completion of the full dissertation. This is often a great help on the occasion of the viva voce examination, since it helps to establish the credibility of the research. In addition, once the dissertation has been examined and (hopefully) passed, the student will often want to try to find a publisher who is prepared to publish the entire dissertation. There are some publishers who specialize in this type of publication. However, the prior storage of the dissertation on an open access database such as EthOS may have a deleterious effect on the likelihood of publication. An investigation of this issue was conducted by Brown and Sadler (2010). The research suggested that there were some concerns about the system, both on the part of university staff and students, and also of some publishers. Supervisors in universities had some concerns that open access storage might affect publication. Some students shared this concern. In addition, there were some publishers who thought that it could possibly affect their decision to publish.

Journal indexes and abstracting databases

Google™Scholar (2011) is a popular method for searching the Web, in order to access a wide range of academic material such as scholarly journal articles, monographs and books, research theses and papers. It provides access to a very large number of academic journals, both from North America and Europe. It enables you to obtain information on the location of academic sources, and in some cases to download paper copies of articles and other materials. A valuable aspect of Google™Scholar is that it enables you to obtain data on the number of times an article has been cited, and also gives you information on articles which are in some way connected to the article for which you have been searching.

There are available a considerable number of abstracting and indexing services aimed at academics and research students. SciVerse® Scopus (Elsevier B.V. 2011) provides bibliographic information and citations for academic articles from nearly 17,000 journals in the broad subject areas of the sciences and social sciences. This service will identify scholarly articles in approximately the same area as the article selected. It will also calculate the number of times an article has been cited in other scholarly publications. SciVerse® Scopus will also identify the names of other academics who are working in a particular field. The scale of its database is considerable. The journals represented are drawn from approximately 5000 different academic journals; and approaching four million academic conference papers are stored in its archives.

The following organizations also provide indexing and abstracting services. The Social Sciences Citation Index® (Thomson Reuters 2011c) is part of the Web of Science® facility, and provides bibliographic and citation information from nearly 2500 academic journals in the area of the social sciences. Apart from facilitating the identification of articles, and providing data on citation rates, it also enables the student to link together the processes of finding articles, writing a dissertation, and constructing a list of references. PsycINFO®, produced by the American Psychological Association (2011), is a database of literature on psychology, from the early part of the nineteenth century up to the contemporary period. It includes a range of bibliographic information, but does not include full text documents. Education Abstracts, produced by EBSCO (2011), collects data from nearly 700 journals in the broad area of educational studies. It is worth noting, however, in relation to bibliographic databases, that they generally concentrate on enabling you to identify articles and other data, but do not normally provide a wide range of full text material. To acquire this, you would need to use the academic library, or libraries, of which you are a member.

Key terms

Blog: a blog is a web-based diary, series of comments, or journal, often structured around a broad theme, to which contributors add 'postings'.
Boolean logic: in this context a system of conducting an electronic search which enables you to broaden or narrow the subject of the search.
Grey literature: any document which is produced outside of the normal process of commercial publishers.
Pre-publishing: making available an article, usually in an open-access, electronic forum, in order to speed up accessibility to readers, when the normal publishing process may be rather time-consuming.

Repository: an electronic database of theses and publications, often in a university, which stores the research output of academics and researchers of that institution. The materials are often made available on an open-access basis.

RSS (Rich Site Summary): a means of receiving regular updates from websites of your choice, as they are amended.

Wiki: a wiki is a connected series of web pages whose content may be amended by a group of people working together.

Key questions

1   When you are selecting articles for your literature review, are more recently published articles going to be more desirable than older articles?
2   What effect do you think the trend towards pre-prints and e-prints will have on the choice of literature for a review?
3   What effect do you think the university repository movement may have on the ability of student researchers to get their research published?

Key reading

Dochartaigh, N.O. (2007) *Internet Research Skills: How to Do your Literature Search and Find Research Information Online*. London: Sage.

Harris, R.A. (2011) *Using Sources Effectively: Strengthening Your Writing and Avoiding Plagiarism*, 3rd edn. Glendale, CA: Pyrczac Publishing.

Pau, M.L. (2008) *Preparing Literature Reviews: Qualitative and Quantitative Approaches*, 3rd edn. Glendale, CA: Pyrczac Publishing.

Pyrczak, F. (2008) *Evaluating Research in Academic Journals: A Practical Guide to Realistic Evaluation*, 4th edn. Glendale, CA: Pyrczac Publishing.

Shaw, M.D. (2007) *Mastering Online Research: A Comprehensive Guide to Effective and Efficient Search Strategies*. Cincinnati, OH: Writers Digest Books.

4

How to select literature for inclusion

Summary • Learning outcomes • Criteria for inclusion • Which literature contributes most to the field? • Methodology of the article • Writing style • Recency • Validity of arguments • Objectivity of approach • Is the author a noted scholar? • Key terms • Key questions • Key reading

Summary

There is often such a wealth of potential literature available for a literature review, that difficult choices have to be made about what to include and what to discard. This chapter examines some of the criteria which you can use to decide which articles or other pieces of writing to include in the review. It explores such issues as citation rates, peer review, the methodology of the article, and the recency of the publication. The chapter also analyses the way in which literature can fit in with, and contribute to, the overall line of argument of a dissertation or piece of research writing.

Learning outcomes

After reading this chapter you should be able to do the following:

- Identify a range of criteria which you can use for selecting literature for your dissertation.

- Understand the ways in which academics tend to evaluate the quality of scholarly writing.
- Appreciate the types of qualitative and quantitative measures by which academics rate research writing.

Criteria for inclusion

It is very difficult to be absolutely prescriptive about something as complex as a literature review. Indeed, this also applies to the far wider task of researching and writing an entire research dissertation. It is not a mechanistic task which can be easily reduced to a few simple items on a checklist. Yet that is often what I am trying to do in this book! My readers would probably be very dissatisfied with me if I did not at least attempt to give some precise advice to help them. However, I simply wish to point out that the writing of a literature review is ultimately a creative activity into which the writer has an enormous input. There are many decisions to take, concerning which it is simply not possible to make precise judgements about in advance. Students often ask me very directed questions about whether a particular journal article is suitable for inclusion, or what type of literature they should discuss. I am sure that sometimes they are not very happy with my answer, as I talk round the subject and then may seem to sit on the fence and not give them precise advice. But what I am trying to do is to explain the various factors which need to be taken into account in taking a decision, and then try to steer the student towards making their own decision. I believe that this encourages you to become an autonomous thinker, who has confidence in his or her own academic decisions.

It is also worth mentioning that academics in general are noteworthy for making up their own minds about things, and not simply going along with what may seem to be the accepted way of doing things. If we were to show a group of academics some journal articles and ask them for an opinion on which should be included and which excluded from a literature review, and for their reasons, I feel fairly confident that we would get different reasons from each academic. This is not a bad thing, but it simply means that you need to be aware that however you decide to approach your literature review, you need to be prepared to justify and explain your decisions. When ultimately you have to defend these decisions in your dissertation viva, remember that there are many different ways you could have approached your writing, and the examiners simply wish to understand how you came to your decisions. In this chapter, therefore, I will try to set out many of the different criteria it is possible to employ, when selecting literature for your review, but ultimately the choice will be yours.

Do not select all the literature on a subject

It is very easy to be rather indiscriminate in selecting the literature for a review. When writing a dissertation, there are always time pressures of various kinds, and there is often a temptation to put any article which seems at all relevant into the literature review chapter. However, it is important to remember that there should be a strategy for the review, and that the strategy which you select is a reflection of the particular approach which you take for the dissertation.

It is always advisable to take into account, at all times, the people who will read your literature review. A dissertation is in many ways an artistic and literary creation. Just as a novel, a poem, a play or even a painting, will be read or looked at by a wide variety of people, your dissertation will probably be read many times by a variety of people in the future. Of course, in the immediate future there will be your supervisors, and then the examiners, but after that many others will read all or parts of your dissertation. It will be placed in a repository, and many future students will consult it to get ideas for their research, and to gain an understanding of how a dissertation should be structured if it is to meet the required standards.

You are therefore writing for all of these people, and it is important to keep them in mind. If the structure of your dissertation is easily understandable; if your arguments are logical and easy to follow, and if your readers can move easily from one part of a chapter to another, without losing your train of thought, then you will be likely to have written a good dissertation. In terms of the literature review, therefore, it should not be an amorphous mass of assorted literature and references, but from the first paragraph, the reader should be able to easily follow the plan which you have developed. They should quickly appreciate the way your mind was working, when you planned the review. In order that you can help your future readers, and make your overall strategy clear and transparent, you need in effect, to put signposts in your chapter, to make it clear to the reader, the logical direction in which your arguments will evolve.

Good practice

When writing the review chapter, try to put linking sentences in the review, to indicate the structure to the reader. For example, at the beginning of the chapter you might write: *The overall presentation of the literature in this chapter is sequential, with the oldest literature being treated first, and the most recent literature last. This applies to each section of the chapter.*

In a dissertation concerned with Knowledge and the Curriculum, you might continue to write: *The first section of this chapter will*

> *examine briefly some of the classical writers who have had an influence upon the philosophy of the curriculum. In the second section, we will continue with an analysis of the so-called 'sociology of knowledge' perspective, and the key thinkers who contributed to that approach.*
>
> In this way, the reader begins to appreciate the way in which your thinking is progressing. Towards the end of the review, you might add another signpost: *Finally, we will now analyze the particular contribution made to the history of knowledge, by the French philosopher Michel Foucault.*
>
> These kind of signposts mean that the reader should ideally never be confused by the dissertation, and should be able to follow the literature review from one logical step to another.

Your selection of literature will therefore need to be conditioned by the way in which you choose to present your arguments to your reader. You will select the types of literature which enable you to link together your arguments with the type of signposts indicated above. Ultimately there is no absolutely correct choice of literature. There may be one or two key publications, which, for various reasons, could scarcely be omitted, because of their commonly conceded importance to the field. However, other than that, you yourself are creating a literary, academic work, and it is your decision on the selection of literature which really counts. It is, arguably, less the particular choices which matter, but the way in which you integrate them into an overall structure which matters. It is less the decisions you make which are particularly significant, but the way in which you justify them.

Nature of the publishing source

While the author and the subject matter of a reference may be the prime factors in evaluating the relevance of a publication, the nature of the publishing source may also be a factor. There are several reasons for this. Publishers inevitably specialize in certain kinds of works, and hence develop a reputation in that area. Some publishers, for example, specialize in the publication of research monographs, which, while not attaining necessarily large circulations, will have a reputation for the nature of the research on which they are based. Other publishers specialize in different types of academic works, including the publication of a wide range of academic journals. While the nature of the publisher is not an absolute determining factor in the quality or intellectual content of a book or article, there a connection by implication. For example, if an edited book comes from a publishing house with a long tradition in publishing monographs based on thorough empirical research, some of that history will attach itself to the book by implication and association. Even though someone may never have read the book, they will still probably make assumptions about the quality of the research and writing, based upon similar books they may have read from the same publishing house. There is no logic or rationality to this, but nevertheless, we all do tend to make these kinds of assumptions. We cannot read everything which is published, and so we do tend to categorize material based on such factors as the publisher.

Nevertheless, there is a kind of rationality in this way of thinking. If a publisher tends to specialize in a certain type of academic output, whether textbooks, research monographs, or scholarly journals, they have staff who are experts in these fields, and also forms of thorough editorial control. They are therefore to a considerable extent, arbiters of academic quality, and students, researchers and academics have some justification in considering the publisher, along with other factors, in deciding whether or not to select a book from the wide range available.

Now the publisher of a source will not be evident in the text of your dissertation, as you will normally only cite the author's surname, year of publication, and perhaps the page number in your actual text. However, in the case of books it will be noted in the list of references at the end of the dissertation. It will not normally be noted for journals, although some more knowledgeable readers will be aware of the publisher of an individual journal. Examiners will certainly look down the list of references at the end of a dissertation, and note the names of publishers. They will probably be aware of many of the publications and authors, but in some cases that will not be the case. Then they will inevitably be guided by the names of the author and of the publisher. If they do not know the name of the author of a particular publication, then the name of the publisher will influence their judgement. One might perhaps summarize this issue by suggesting that the names of publishers may not perhaps be a major factor in determining the quality of a dissertation, but nevertheless they do help to create something of the academic atmosphere of a piece of work.

Is the source peer-reviewed?

We have explored the system of peer review in relation to journal articles, although it is useful to reflect upon the reasons for the development of this system of quality control in terms of academic writing. It is very difficult to make absolute judgements about the quality of academic writing, indeed perhaps of any kind of writing. Certainly, in the area of creative writing, there are many examples of novels and other books, which have not been thought very worthy initially, only later to become bestsellers. In terms of academic writing, it is possible to delineate certain criteria which are useful in forming judgements about academic quality, and we will examine these further in later chapters. However, it is in the application of criteria where academics often tend to disagree. For example, in a qualitative research study, the researcher may have used a purposive sample of eight respondents. One academic may feel that this was an acceptable size of sample, while another may feel that it was too small. There is no absolute way in which to resolve such a dispute. In addition, this kind of genuine difference of opinion can be replicated with many other different aspects of a piece of research. In terms then of trying to decide what is an acceptable piece of work and what is not, we are left in an almost impossible situation. All we can do is to look for some kind of consensus. This is, in reality, the ultimate purpose of the peer-review system. We are not trying to achieve complete agreement between two or three reviewers. It would be very unlikely if we achieved this, and even if we did, we might well wonder whether we would be fully justified in taking too much notice of it.

Hence, although we are not realistically expecting too much of the peer-review system, it does achieve a number of important goals for us. First of all, the system ensures that several people have read a piece of research, and commented upon it. The very fact that this will happen to a piece of academic writing means that the writer will have done his or her utmost to achieve as high a quality piece of work as possible, as they will not want their work to be unduly criticized within the public domain. Second, the system of peer review should be able to create a situation where two or more reviewers achieve, if not complete agreement, at least a form of consensus about the quality or otherwise of the work. This consensus subsequently enables the writer to make amendments and improvements to the work. The process will often reveal to the writer some aspects of their work that they had not previously considered. Finally, there is the perhaps slightly philosophical advantage that the peer-review system places academic work in the public domain. Research cannot normally be hidden away from public scrutiny, and this tends to ensure that most research writing adheres to the accepted conventions. Therefore, when we are selecting literature for a review, if we know that it has been peer-reviewed, we do at least know that the above quality checks will have been applied. It may not be a perfect piece of research, but we know that at least it has been subject to a reasonable degree of checking by informed peers.

The value of the peer-review process

Even though there may be no absolute way in which we can judge the quality of research, the peer-review process does provide a number of very valuable checks and balances upon published research.

When submitting the article to discussion and analysis by peer reviewers, the writer can often receive suggestions for improving the article. This willingness to concede that improvements may not only be possible, but desirable, is a cornerstone of the peer-review process. It hopefully leads to a spirit of cooperation in the academic world, where scholars are happy to work together in the pursuance of higher standards of research and academic writing.

Importantly, the review process enables arguments and data analysis to be checked by other academics who are familiar with the field and the methodology. Sometimes it could happen that the principles of the data analysis are perfectly correct, but the article contains errors in calculations or statistics. The review process often enables these to be corrected.

The review process also enhances public confidence in the research process. In a world where research findings are often used to support or justify policy decisions in different areas, it is important that the public is reassured about the research process. If findings have clearly been subject to checking and verification by impartial academics, then this should go some way to providing that confidence in the process.

How often has the source been cited?

Increasingly, there are attempts within the academic world to evaluate the worth of research articles in an objective way. One of these ways has been to try to quantify the number of times an individual piece of research writing has been cited in other sources. The assumption is that the greater the frequency of citation, and particularly citation in journals with a strong academic reputation, then this is an indication of the quality of the article, or of the esteem in which the article and author are held. There are various ways in which it is possible to gain a measure of the citation frequency of an article, and we will look at these later. It is probably, however, unrealistic to assume that you will try to check the citation frequency of every journal article which you are anticipating using in your literature review. You will have so many different aspects of your research on your mind, as you write your dissertation, that there will almost certainly not be the time to do this. Nevertheless, it is an increasingly important measure of research quality, and it is worth perhaps having some idea of it, in relation to at least some of the articles you cite or quote from.

However, it is worth noting that there are some difficulties and possible inconsistencies with the whole approach. The entire 'research industry' is expanding very rapidly, and with it there is a large increase in the number of academic journals. An academic author therefore has a wider and wider choice of potential articles to draw from when selecting articles to cite in his or her writing. The probability that an individual article will be selected for citation is thus reduced. This remains the situation even given the expansion in the variety of different electronic search mechanisms which are available. In addition, your institutional library will simply not be able to take out subscriptions to all of the journals which ideally you would like to read. The increasing number of journals is an important factor here, as are the limitations on library funds. As a student you can always request that your library takes out a subscription to a journal, but this may not always be possible. The advent of open access publishing may have an effect on citation rates. If articles are freely available, then other things being equal, it seems likely that they may have higher citation rates. There are, however, other factors operating here. Open access journals are financed in a variety of different ways, for example. Although these are different to the financing of conventional journals, they may still have an effect on the likelihood of publication of an individual article, and hence its rate of citation.

There are a number of different measures which are used to estimate the quality of individual articles and journals, and also to judge the collected scholarly output of an academic. The **H index** (or Hirsch Index) relates to the output of an individual academic. It provides a measure of the overall output in terms of the quantity of research, research articles and research monographs; and also links this to an estimate of the extent to which this output has been publicly recognized within the academic community through the citation process. In terms of the latter, it incorporates a measure of the number of times each article has been cited in the publications of other scholars. The H index can be used to measure the academic output of a single researcher, or of a group of researchers working in the same field. Inevitably, it can also be used to compare the output of different individuals. However, in this case, it only really has some validity if it is employed to compare individuals who are working in the same research field.

A related measure, but one whose focus is upon the journal rather than the academic author, is the **Journal Impact Factor**. The impact factor provides an estimate of the significance, status or importance of an academic journal, within a particular circumscribed academic field. It is calculated based upon the number of times articles published in a journal are cited in other academic journals. There are various databases which compute impact factors, and from which they can easily be retrieved. Journal Citation Reports, published by Thomson Reuters, computes journal impact factors for all the journals which it monitors.

The Web of Knowledge™ (Thomson Reuters 2011d) generates a great deal of data on citations. It analyses over 20,000 academic journals and over 100,000 academic conference proceedings. It provides access to the Arts and Humanities Citation Index, and the Social Sciences Citation Index.

Which literature contributes most to the field?

In a sense there is no objective and precise answer to this question. You will need to establish your own line of reasoning and sequence of arguments for your dissertation, and then select the literature which best appears to substantiate your arguments. Ideally, you should be able to justify each article and other research document which you include in your literature review. They should be there because they fit in to the overall plan of your research report.

However, it is possible to justify the inclusion of an article in a more objective manner. Some databases publish a variety of forms of statistics which enable you to make quantitatively informed decisions about the relevance or importance of research articles. The Social Science Research Network (Social Science Electronic Publishing 2011) consists of a number of different integrated networks and databases in the social sciences, whose purpose is to encourage the fastest possible spread of new research findings and results. The network has an electronic library consisting of nearly 350,000 abstracts of articles, and nearly 300,000 articles and documents, which can largely be downloaded. Interestingly, the Social Science Research Network maintains a list of the articles which have most frequently been downloaded from the journals indexed by the research network. This provides you with a measurable justification for selecting a certain article for inclusion. Other databases provide useful information which can be used to evaluate articles. Zetoc (University of Manchester, 2011), for example, enables you to search the Tables of Contents of about 20,000 academic journals, and about 16,000 conference proceedings at the British Library.

Methodology of the article

It is certainly not necessary that the articles which you select for your literature review should have the same methodological approach. This would probably be too restrictive for you, and would unnecessarily limit the number of articles which you could realistically use. However, when you read the articles you are considering for inclusion, you will certainly devote time to evaluating the methodology, and this will become one of the factors in deciding whether or not to include it. In some circumstances, the methodology of the article may be a crucial factor in your decision-making.

As a general rule in writing about research, it is very useful to be able to cite articles which have employed a methodology similar to yours. This is not to say that your research design should be exactly based upon that in another piece of research, but that the broad themes are similar. One of the reasons for this is that it acts as a form of justification for what you have done. Let us say, for example, that you are employing interview research as your basic research design, and decide to use a stratified random sampling technique in order to select university students to interview. This technique is usually employed where you wish to ensure that the overall features of, say, the university student population are represented in proportion in the final choice of a sample. In order to justify and illustrate this approach you might reasonably set out to find other examples of research which have adopted this approach. Such research articles could help your dissertation in a variety of ways. They might raise questions about research procedure and ethics, which you could use as the starting point for a discussion about aspects of your own research. They could also discuss the reasons for selecting the particular sampling procedure, which would help you in evaluating the success or otherwise of your decisions about research design. Overall, then, it may be very useful to have at least some articles for inclusion which have adopted a similar methodological approach to your own research.

To take a contrary view for the moment, there is also an argument for selecting articles which have investigated a similar topic to your own research, but have adopted a variety of different research designs and methodologies. The reason for this is that they can shed a different light upon the topic, and examine different facets of the same type of research question. They can thus provide you with opportunities to compare and contrast your own research with other possible approaches. This can help you in the process of articulating the reasons for adopting your particular approach.

Other circumstances where the methodology of an article can be important is in a situation where you might have chosen a research design which is rather unusual. It may be a perfectly acceptable research design, but it may simply be less frequently employed. One example may be the use of life history research as a methodology. It would be perfectly possible to construct a dissertation, even at doctoral level, around a study of the life histories of a very small number of respondents, or even of simply one respondent. This approach can lead to a very interesting dissertation, with extremely detailed and rich data. However, one of the difficulties with such research, is that it is not necessarily very easy to generalize from the data. It can be difficult to establish an argument that the findings from the extremely small sample have a wider applicability to other people and other contexts. On the one hand, you might wish to try to make out a case that the particular respondent or respondents chosen are typical of others in the same profession or same social situation. This would perhaps better enable you to generalize more widely from your findings. On the other hand, you might want to argue that your respondent represents an extreme or unusual case, which can illustrate specific features of their social context, by virtue of the very fact that they are unusual in some way.

Other examples of methodologies which might be considered a little unusual would be ethnomethodology and some aspects of phenomenological research. These are perfectly legitimate approaches to certain research questions, but it might be very useful to support their choice, by reference to a range of literature which has adopted the same approach. It is also worth bearing in mind that a body of supporting literature can be very useful in convincing an external examiner that you have approached questions of methodology in a systematic and logical way. In a perfect world, external examiners for research dissertations would be familiar with every aspect of the dissertation, including the subject matter and the methodology adopted. However, this may not be the situation in every case. External examiners may be appointed primarily because of their academic background in the subject matter of the research. While no doubt being aware of the methodological approach, they may not be totally familiar with it, if it were a particularly unusual approach. In such a situation, it would no doubt strengthen your case considerably, if you could point to a body of literature which had employed this approach.

Comparing the research methodologies of two articles

This is an exercise which you may need to conduct on several occasions in your literature review. In order to make an effective comparison, it is perhaps easier to compare two articles which involve research on broadly the same topic. It is also easier to compare them if the methodologies are roughly within the same perspective; that is, they are both within an interpretive perspective or a positivist perspective. If not, then there may be some confusion because of the different expectations and norms with regard to, say, sample size, and sampling strategy.

It is usual, for example, for there to be a smaller sample in interpretive research than in survey research. In comparing them, one could not really say a great deal about the different sample sizes, only perhaps discuss the appropriateness of the sample size to the respective research design. On the other hand, there may be more to discuss, if you were analyzing the sample sizes in two pieces of interpretive research.

Finally, there is a school of thought among supervisors of dissertations that it is generally a safer option to select a methodology which has been fairly widely employed. Not only is it easier in this case to find journal articles which in terms of methodology are closely connected with your research, but also it is perhaps easier to justify the research design with the examiners of the dissertation. They are more likely to be familiar with your approach, and hence there will usually be less need for justification.

Writing style

The writing style of academic articles and reports of research is fairly consistent and complies generally with the accepted norms of the genre. If the arguments and conclusions of an article are to be clearly understood, then it needs to be written in a fairly formal, precise style. In addition, however, the article would not be published, and hence would not come to the attention of the research community, unless it was written in an accepted style.

Having said this, however, there are still considerable variations in the writing found in academic articles. Some can be fairly convoluted and complex, using many long words and specialist terms. On the other hand, some authors manage to employ a simpler, more straightforward style. There are also some differences of style in academic journal articles which relate to the methodology employed. Some research perspectives such as action research and phenomenology may, for example, develop a slightly different style of writing. However, in general, articles published in academic journals comply with a fairly consistent academic style.

However, it is in grey literature and on some websites that we find writing styles which differ somewhat from the norm. Some websites may employ slightly more informal or colloquial linguistic styles, because they have a target audience which is looking for a more populist presentation style. In addition, some websites may be attempting to disseminate a message which is essentially ideological in nature, and therefore may employ value-laden language. Finally, some aspects of grey literature may employ informal language for magazines or pamphlets. Ultimately you will need to decide for yourself, whether the style of a piece of literature is too informal, or deviates too much from the norm, to be included in your review. It may be that informality of style is not on its own a necessary condition for excluding a piece of literature, since the content of the article may be particularly significant.

Common pitfall

One of the features of good academic writing is that when considering an issue, it tends to examine at least two different viewpoints on the question. Consequently, a fairly balanced picture begins to emerge. When you are writing your literature review, this enables you to weigh up different features of the question, and produce a fair and even-handed analysis.

However, some websites are more concerned with getting you to believe their ideas, than with opening up a balanced debate. Therefore you need to be especially careful with websites which appear to just present one perspective on something, rather than several different points of view.

Recency

It is a commonly held belief that in academic writing, the more recent the references the better. The assumption is that for a good literature review, most of the references should have been published within the last few years. However, we ought to submit this assumption to critical scrutiny. Why is it that we assume more recent is best?

First of all, this assumption might have something to do with the enormous expansion in research activity in recent years. Social science research has become a kind of industry in its own right. We do tend to believe that there is a gradual progression of knowledge. As the centuries have passed, we feel that we have become more knowledgeable and also wiser. We feel that this is partly linked to the growth in research activity, and the overall expansion of knowledge to which the human species has access. We assume that more knowledge leads to more wisdom, and a more intelligent approach to organizing our lives and also the world. More research does perhaps lead to more knowledge; but whether that additional knowledge leads to wiser understanding of the world is another question. There is also a danger that the expansion of research also brings with it a certain repetition. Since research output is closely linked to the career progression of academics, there is a great motivation to publish more and more articles in more and more journals. It could be argued that this results to some extent in a reworking of old themes. It would be too presumptive to suggest that the overall standard of academic articles has fallen with the exponential growth of academic publications in recent years. However, it might also be rash to presume that the more recent articles are necessarily better, or have more profound insights than those published 20 or 30 years ago. We need to have more precise and insightful criteria to judge articles and research than simply the recency of the article.

There is also another dimension to the recency or age of research articles. The general approach to social science research and in particular, to research methodology, to some extent goes in cycles. For example, in the 1960s, there was a greater preponderance of positivistic, quantitative studies in education. This approach was gradually replaced with a growing emphasis upon interpretive and qualitative studies. Certainly qualitative studies are more fashionable now than they used to be in the 1960s. Therefore, an exclusive focus upon only the most recent articles in a particular area of educational or social science research, would almost inevitably lead to a certain bias in terms of methodology. This is not to say that recency is not a valuable criterion to use in terms of selecting articles, but it would probably be unwise to give it excessive importance.

Validity of arguments

When you select an article to include in your literature review, it will already have been through a number of quality controls which should to some extent reassure you of its worth. If it was published in a reputable academic journal, then you know that it will have been peer-reviewed, and proofread. The editor of the journal will also have read it. If it has been joint authored, then at least two colleagues are in accord with the general arguments of the article. You can also examine the institutions from which the authors of the article, and also the editorial board members, come, as an indicator of quality.

Nevertheless, you should also read articles yourself, in order to feel satisfied that the arguments are well expressed and are valid. You should also verify that the general tone of the discussion in the article, and of the arguments, fits well with the overall trend of your dissertation, and of the contribution to knowledge which you are seeking to make.

There is another way in which you can reassure yourself about the quality of an article, and indeed about the validity of the arguments which it contains. This is whether the article has been obtained from a database which has strict quality standards in terms of archiving a particular journal or article. ERIC, the Education Resources Information Center (Institute of Education Sciences 2011), is such a database. ERIC is a very large database, containing a wide range of research materials, and other education literature. It indexes over one thousand education-related journals, and nearly one million journal articles. It also indexes just over half-a-million items which are not derived from journals. Of the journals which are indexed on ERIC's records, most are serious academic journals which are peer-reviewed. ERIC has comprehensive selection criteria, particularly in relation to journals which are indexed. When accepting a journal for indexing, ERIC considers such issues as the rejection rate of the journal, the review procedures and the composition of the editorial board. If you therefore decide to access an article from a journal indexed by such a body, then this provides an additional level of quality screening, and further evidence of methodological validity.

Objectivity of approach

Whenever any researcher or academic writes a research article, their writing will almost inevitably be influenced by many factors other than the attempt to present a balanced, objective approach. Every one of us who works in the field of academic work or research has had a different education. Even if two people have attended the same school and university, and even if they have studied exactly the same subjects with exactly the same teachers (all of which is very unlikely), they would still have had a very different educational experience. They would each have gained very different things from their education. They would have consulted different books when writing their assignments, and would have worked harder at some parts of their courses than at others. But the most important difference would have derived from the way in which they interacted with what they were taught. As they each had different personalities and intellects, they would have interpreted what they were taught in very different ways. They would have gained different things from their teaching, and in their own minds would have placed more emphasis on some aspects of their courses than on others. At the end of the day, they would have developed subtly different world views. As adults, they would look at the world in a slightly different way. We could say that they had developed a different ideological perspective. In many cases the ideological differences between people may be very minor. In other cases, a person may, as a result of their education or upbringing, develop a distinctive political or religious viewpoint, which they come to hold unshakeably. If they are a lecturer, they may develop a particular philosophy of education, which they hold so strongly, that they would not normally be dissuaded from it. We could say that all of these different viewpoints represent the different ideological positions held by people.

Within this kind of analysis it is very difficult, if not impossible, for someone to be absolutely objective when they are discussing a research article, or deciding whether to include it in a literature review. Although we may try to be objective, fair and balanced, we are implicitly or explicitly approaching the decision from our own particular academic perspective or ideology. It is very difficult to avoid this accumulated effect of our education and upbringing.

This is not to say that objectivity should not remain a goal in academic research and writing, but merely that we should recognize that, depending perhaps upon our particular philosophical position about these issues, it may remain an unattainable goal. When we are deciding therefore whether to include material in our literature review, we should try to reflect as carefully as possible upon the reasons for our decisions. We should try to be self-reflective, and to analyze as precisely as possible our thought processes. It is then important to do our best to commit these to writing, and to enable the reader to appreciate the nature of our analytic processes.

Within this perspective, therefore, we could argue that objectivity is not truly possible, if we mean by that a completely dispassionate logical process. However, we can also think of objectivity as a process whereby we try to make visible to the world, our thought process. Objectivity then becomes a kind of transparency of thought, whereby we are open and honest about the way we reach our decisions, yet accepting that we may be influenced by a variety of factors.

Is the author a noted scholar?

We mentioned earlier the use of citation frequency as one method for selecting an article for inclusion, and of implicitly forming a judgement about the author of an article. Most writers will try to cite at least some authors whom they regard as being leading figures in their field, and there are a variety of ways in which you might form such a judgement. As a student you will often be guided initially by authors mentioned by your lecturers or supervisors. You will look at reading lists which you are given, and search out books and articles by academics who are mentioned during tutorials. This should provide you with an initial familiarization with some of the key writers. By looking at the lists of references in their articles, you will locate other authors, and probably find that they often cite each other in their writing.

This is probably inevitable, as academics do tend to work in networks. They will meet at conferences, book launches and other events. They will also work together collaboratively on research proposals to attract funding for their institutions. The teams who work on such projects normally come from different universities, and are often international in nature. As they work together in these different ways, they will become aware of each other's work, and this will often be reflected in the citations in their articles. At conferences, academics will listen to accounts of current research, and this will sometimes later be mentioned in their own articles.

As you start to read widely in a particular subject area, you will find that the names of certain authors occur more and more. You will begin to understand the way in which these networks of academics are operating. You will see the names of scholars with whom you are familiar in the lists of editorial board members of journals, for example. It will not take you too long to begin to recognize the academics who are key names in the field you are researching. Many academic articles are also often written jointly by two or more academics, and in their lists of references you will find articles which have thus been jointly selected, and are presumably held in some esteem by the authors collectively. Overall then, although these may be to some extent relatively subjective ways of determining the key figures in a field, they do enable you to begin to map the connections between some of the leading writers. As you then begin to consider your own selection process, you can apply a range of other criteria in deciding who to include in your dissertation.

Criteria for selecting literature for inclusion

The following criteria could be useful when deciding whether or not to include an article in your literature review:

- the nature of the journal publishing the article;
- the peer-review process to which the article was submitted;
- the number of times the article has been cited;
- the way in which the research design and methodology are discussed in the article;
- the date the article was published;
- the quality of the academic writing;
- the reputation of the author(s).

Key terms

H-index: a measure of the scholarly output of an individual academic in terms of both the number of articles published, and the number of citations received by each article.

Journal Impact Factor: a measure of the academic status of a journal based on the number of citations received by articles published in that journal.

Key questions

1 What are the main functions of the peer-review process?
2 What are the main factors causing an increased number of journal articles to be published?
3 What are some of the consequences of open access publishing?

Key reading

Caro, S. (2009) *How to Publish Your PhD: A Practical Guide for the Humanities and Social Sciences*. London: Sage.

Kitchin, R. and Fuller, D. (2005) *The Academic's Guide to Publishing*. London: Sage.

Mounsey, C. (2002) *One Step Ahead: Essays and Dissertations*. Oxford: Oxford University Press.

Parrott, L. (1998) *How to Write Psychology Papers*, 2nd edn. Harlow: Longman.

Pears, R. and Shields, G. (2010) *Cite Them Right: The Essential Referencing Guide*, 8th edn. Basingstoke: Palgrave Macmillan.

5

Analyzing and categorizing the literature critically

Summary • Learning outcomes • Checklist of criteria • Methodology
• Criteria • Key term • Key questions • Key reading

Summary

A good literature review does not simply choose literature, divide it into sections and then describe it. It does all these things, but much more besides. It analyses each piece of research literature, examining its strengths and weaknesses, and considers the validity of its findings. In particular, it discusses the appropriateness of the methodology selected. The review also compares and contrasts articles, seeking points of similarity and difference. It also combines ideas from several articles, looking for ways in which the collected ideas can be used to create fresh insights. This chapter explores some of the ways in which these processes can be carried out, to generate an account which illuminates the research for which the literature review has been written.

Learning outcomes

After reading this chapter you should be able to do the following:

- List the different analytic processes used to discuss the literature in a review.
- Describe the different elements of a research article, which you would subject to analysis.
- Be able to put into practice the various analytic processes discussed in the chapter.

Checklist of criteria

The literature review is one of the most deceptively complex of the various activities involved in writing a dissertation. For many students it is an opportunity, first and foremost, to gather together a large number of references, and show that he or she has read very widely. This is followed by selecting a large number of fairly long quotations, and then briefly discussing those quotations. A good literature review is, however, much more complex than this, and it is the aim of this chapter to help you understand and practise some of the techniques which will enable you to create a good review. Let us begin by listing and discussing briefly, some of these thought processes. We will then examine them in more detail later in the chapter.

Methodology

It is possible to consider a single research topic, and then to look at it from a variety of different perspectives. Each perspective will shed a different light upon the issue, revealing perhaps a different point of view. These perspectives will often be methodological in character. A survey, for example, will usually tell us about the broad themes of a research question, but will not go into any great depth with a research question. Unstructured interviews, on the one hand, will normally provide a great deal of very rich data, which will go into considerable detail on a few aspects of the question. On the other hand, they will not provide the broad picture. By grouping articles according to methodology, you can hence gain a variety of viewpoints on the research issue.

Good practice	

A research issue or problem is seldom simple and straightforward. There are usually many different aspects to it. The only way to understand these different facets is to adopt a range of different research methods. Data collection and analysis methods are different, because they are each designed to address different types of issues. Some look deeply at a question, and some are designed to skim over the surface looking for broad trends. It is good practice to seek out litera- ture which fulfils each of these different approaches, and then you can be more confident that you have explored as many dimensions of the issue as possible.

Content

The subject matter or content of an article is perhaps the logical way in which literature can be categorized. You will need to be flexible, however, in the literature which you accept for your review. You may not be able to locate exactly the type of literature you want, in terms of subject matter. It may be necessary to categorize articles in slightly different ways to those which you anticipated when you first started the dissertation. Nevertheless, we do not live in an ideal world, and your plans will need to be driven, to some extent, by the nature and content of the literature which you uncover. What is important, however, is that you have a structure to your review, even though it may not be the structure which you had initially anticipated.

Controversies

There are arguments, disagreements and differences of opinion in most areas of academic life. This is not necessarily a bad thing at all, but indicates a healthy sense of debate, which at its best can advance the knowledge and understanding which we have about a certain subject. Imagine if everyone agreed about the most eco-friendly way to generate electricity, or the most effective way to cure a patient, or on the best economic policy for the country! Not only would life be very boring, but there would not be that intense discus- sion, which encourages us to re-evaluate our own ideas. It is through that re-assessment of our thinking, that we can make academic progress. Controversies also prompt research. One long-standing debate in psychology is known commonly as the 'nature–nurture' debate. In other words, are we influenced more by our genetic inheritance or by the way we have been brought up? This controversy alone has initiated a great many research studies, trying to resolve a fundamental question of human development. When you are reading your literature try to identify differences of opinion, and then reflect upon the ways in which your own research might fit in to these discussions, and indeed help to resolve them.

Common pitfall

As a general rule, try not to seek out absolute truths in research. You are unlikely to find them, and if you think you have done so, you are likely to be mistaken! This tends to apply when you are carrying out research, and also when you are analyzing research literature. In social science research it is much better to maintain a slight feeling of scepticism and uncertainty. When you think you can safely draw a definite conclusion, try immediately to think of an exception which will make you much less certain. This will tend to lead to more balanced and objective conclusions.

Summarizing

If you consider that a literature review chapter for a doctorate may easily include several hundred individual citations, and that each article (leaving books on one side) may be of about 8000 words, it is easy to see that you will have an enormous amount of information to organize and control. The only way that you will realistically be able to cope with this is if you can, to some extent, summarize the information, and make it more manageable. There are various ways in which you can approach the writing of a synopsis or précis. One of them is to consider each paragraph in the original, and summarize it in a single sentence. Even that would probably leave you with too much information, and therefore you might need to consider a larger section of the original, and then summarize that. It may even be necessary to allow yourself only two or three sentences per article, and reduce each citation to just several lines. You will also need to have a coding mechanism to link your synopsis back to the original. At any rate, by doing this you should be in a position to categorize your literature into meaningful sections.

Synthesizing

When you begin a detailed reading of the literature you have selected, you may well recognize features that articles or books have in common. Indeed, although they may be different in terms of methodology, the broad approaches used may enable them to be linked together in a meaningful way. For example, you may identify some articles which use a life history approach; others which describe themselves as oral history; while others adopt the label biographical research. In terms of methodology, there may in fact only be rather slight differences between them, and it may be useful to link them together, exploring the aspects that this approach to research have in common. For example, this type of person-centred, historical research often tries to synthesize the lives of individuals, with the broader trends taking place in society during their lifetimes. Synthesis of this kind can be a very useful strategy in literature analysis.

Analyzing

Equally, it may often be possible to sub-divide an article or research report in terms of its subject matter or methodology. Let us suppose, for example, that a research study employed an ethnographic approach. Such a methodology might employ a variety of data collection measures including interviews, field diaries and participant observation. By dissecting those aspects of the study which used one of these approaches, it might be possible to link the article with another using the same methodology. In other words, you do not have to consider an article just as it is presented, but you can analyze it into its constituent parts, or perhaps identify elements which you consider important. You can then use these elements to develop connections with other articles.

Themes

There are many different social themes which may emerge in an article. Although an article may be focused on a substantive topic such as school management, and may have a specific data collection strategy such as focus groups, there may be other aspects which are important to the research. For example, gender may emerge as a theme, in the context of the relative numbers of male and female head teachers; ethnicity may be a theme in terms of the ethnic background of head teachers in racially-mixed schools; and age may be a theme in the context of the average age of applicants for headships. In other words, one can raise questions about a research report which go beyond the key issues which might be discussed in the abstract.

Evaluating

It is very important when you read a published journal article, that you adopt a critical frame of mind. By that I do not mean that you are necessarily looking for things to 'criticize'. What you should try to do, however, is to cultivate a sceptical attitude about all the propositions and assertions in the article. For example, if the writer claims that the sample size of 20 is appropriate to this research method and research design, you should ask yourself whether you are convinced about this. Has the writer presented sufficient evidence and argument to support this contention? When the writer presents the quotations from the data for analysis, you could ask yourself whether the grounds for the selection of quotations is made clear. Why were these quotations selected and not others from the transcripts? What criteria were used? Is the selection process discussed in the article? Is it acknowledged that there was a selection procedure to choose the data for inclusion in the article? It is therefore not a matter of disbelieving the author, but of asking oneself questions about the procedures and thought processes used in planning and conducting the research. Such a 'critical' frame of mind is part of the process of evaluating research reports.

Comparing different views on a subject

It is no bad thing for one academic to disagree with another. Providing it is based upon an honest and rational assessment of the issue, it is perfectly reasonable to have a difference of opinion. Disagreements on an academic issue may never be resolved in reality, simply because there does not exist sufficient evidence to weigh up, in order to come to a decisive conclusion. Even if there is considerable further data, it may not be of such a nature as to decisively sway the argument one way or another. Where those disputing an issue address that issue using calm, logical reasoning, it can lead to a much better understanding of the issue.

Sometimes, however, people try to support their view by drawing in apparent support from other people. They may argue that 'my idea must be true because person X or organization Y believe it to be true' (where X and Y are commonly supposed to be experts in the matter). This kind of argument may to some extent support the original proposition, but it does not improve the argument, and certainly not prove it to be true. What is needed is fresh, additional evidence. When reading articles, therefore, rather than being swayed by one particular argument, look at a range of contrasting views, and try to decide which you prefer on purely rational grounds.

Taking notes

Throughout the different processes in this checklist, it is very useful to compile notes as your ideas develop. As you synthesize ideas in two or more articles, or cast a critical, evaluative eye over them, you need to maintain succinct, but accurate notes on your thoughts. These notes will become crucial when you finally start to do the actual writing. Everyone has their own system for taking notes, but however you compile them, you should try to combine the processes of reading, followed by analysis and reflection, note taking and then more reading. If you feel that you need a strategy for note taking, then the Mind Map® approach (see Buzan 2010) may be useful.

Criteria

Methodology as a criterion

A useful means of finding literature which adopts the same methodological approach is to consult the professional association which specializes in that particular methodology or research orientation. For example, sociologists and psychologists have their own professional associations, and these organizations often act as a channel for new research in those areas. Very often too, they sponsor or publish academic journals which specialize in certain areas of, say, sociological or psychological research. The Action Learning and Action Research Association (ALARA 2010) is an example of an association with a very precise remit. It exists to support and advocate the use of action learning and action research. It tries to encourage the key principles of action research, that is a collaborative approach to try to resolve issues at a local level, in the workplace, organizations and educational institutions. Members of ALARA come from a variety of contexts, but are all broadly interested in the capacity of action learning and action research to transform society, albeit starting at the micro level. ALARA sponsors a number of different journals which provide opportunities for both authors to publish their research, and for students to locate articles all linked by a commitment to this type of research. The journals are *The Action Learning and Action Research Journal* (ALARj); *Systemic Practice and Action Research*; *Action Research*; *The International Journal of Action Research*; and *Action Research International*. ALARA also publishes The Action Research Case Study monographs, which enable authors to discuss their research in considerable detail. The monographs are refereed, and hence if you consult them or include them in your review, you would have confidence in the process to which they had been submitted. ALARA also publishes reviews of recently published books in the area of action learning and action research, which are a help to students trying to follow the latest literature. In short, then, this kind of professional association can be a great help in identifying works which use a particular methodology or theoretical approach. They can help you identify a body of research literature which, by sharing a common theme, can give structure to your literature review.

Another example of a professional organization is the American Sociological Association (ASA 2011). This was established in 1905, and exists to support and further the work of professional sociologists. It sponsors a number of major journals which would be very useful in identifying articles in the sociological field in general, or indeed in more specialist areas. The principal journal of the association is arguably the *American Sociological Review* (2011) which was first published in 1936. It has an international reputation and publishes articles on all aspects of sociological research. The website of the ASA, for all of its journals, provides a list of selected articles which would be very useful for students trying to identify further publications in an area. Other journals published by the ASA include *Social Psychology Quarterly*, *Teaching Sociology*, and *Sociology of Education*.

Therefore, when you are writing your literature review, if you wish to construct an analysis focused on methodological issues, it can be very useful to consult the websites of professional associations. They can enable you to identify articles using a particular methodological perspective such as action research, or perhaps a broader approach such as sociological research. Such associations also usually organize academic conferences in their subject area, and afterwards publish conference proceedings which can be useful in helping you to be up-to-date in the content of your review. The Australian Psychological Society (2011), for example, does this. The Society also publishes a number of journals including the *Australian Journal of Psychology*, the *Australian Psychologist*, the *Clinical Psychologist*, and the *Australian and New Zealand Journal of Organizational Psychology*. The Australian Psychological Society also enables members to publish details of their latest published research, and this can be a valuable resource for researchers wanting to monitor the latest developments in psychological research.

Content as a criterion

When you are classifying the literature to be included in the literature review, according to subject matter, there are again a number of research-oriented subject associations which can provide source materials, or ideas for categorizing literature. In the case of educational research, the British Educational Research Association (BERA 2011) is an influential body, and potentially very useful to students and researchers. Education is an interdisciplinary subject and draws upon contributions and expertise from areas such as psychology, sociology, economics, history, politics, management and philosophy. This has created new disciplines such as the philosophy of education and the management of education. BERA acts as a collective organization to link together academics and researchers who are working in any of these fields. This eclectic approach is reflected in the journal sponsored by BERA, the *British Educational Research Journal*. The general purpose of BERA is ultimately to improve the quality of education, through supporting educational research. It encourages the development of an intellectual community committed to the furtherance of our understanding of educational processes. Of interest to students is that each year BERA sponsors a Dissertation Award for the best doctoral dissertation in education, produced in a British university.

BERA also has links with other leading educational research organizations, including the European Educational Research Association (2011), often abbreviated to EERA. This European organization was founded in 1994, and links approximately 20 different research organizations. Of particular interest to students is that it sponsors an Emerging Researchers Group for those who are currently registered for doctoral research, or who have completed their doctorate within the last six years. There is also an annual Emerging Researchers Conference. This initiative helps research students to make contact with other young researchers across Europe, and in principle, to identify projects, reports and publications which might be of interest for their dissertations and literature reviews. Possibly of more significance, are the approximately 25 research networks established by EERA. In terms of subject areas, these networks reach right across the whole area of educational research, including such research subjects as Vocational Education and Training, Social Justice and

Intercultural Education, and Research in Higher Education. These networks would provide an opportunity for you to contact researchers, both new and experienced, in a field of interest to you, and potentially to identify new articles and publications. More than that, however, discussions with such researchers may generate ideas for categorizing your literature review. EERA is also open to suggestions for new networks, and there is a mechanism to submit proposals.

Finally, in the area of educational research, the National Foundation for Educational Research in England and Wales, usually known simply as the NFER (2011), occupies a significant position. It is an independent research organization with research expertise in many areas of education. It publishes the journal *Educational Research*, which was founded in 1958. The many research reports which it publishes could be a very useful resource for a literature review.

Controversies in a subject

A considerable amount of research is centred around controversies in a subject. There are many controversies in research in the social sciences, often because it is in the nature of the discipline that it is difficult to justify taking an absolute position with regard to an issue. One area of conflict is in the examination of doctoral theses. Most doctoral theses are examined with some form of oral examination. The research student has to present their dissertation before a panel of experienced academics. Usually there must be at least one examiner from the university where the student has carried out their research, and one examiner from a different university. They are known respectively as the 'internal' and 'external' examiner.

Each university will have a standard process for the appointment of the examiners. It will often involve approval by a small committee of experienced academics and researchers. The proposed examiners, both internal and external, will probably, however, be suggested by the student's supervisors. There will usually be limitations upon the number of times an external examiner may be selected by a university to be a doctoral examiner. In most cases the examiners will be approved by applying criteria such as the number of times they have acted as doctoral examiners, and their knowledge of the subject matter of the dissertation. The latter may need to be demonstrated by the research publications of the proposed examiners.

The decision as to who to propose as examiners for their research student is clearly a very crucial decision for supervisors. They would naturally hope that whoever they propose, would, if accepted, be supportive to their student, even if they did not think the dissertation was the best piece of work they had ever seen. However, so complex is a research dissertation, that it is probably unrealistic to suppose that different academics would all have the same opinion about it. Different academics, no matter how experienced in the subject and in questions of research, may perfectly sincerely come to different conclusions about the quality of a dissertation. This makes it very difficult for supervisors to decide on who to propose as examiners. The issue is particularly difficult with regard to the external examiners, since the supervisors are not likely to know them very well compared with the internal examiners.

There is a major area of contention inherent in this issue. A research degree candidate would be entitled to be rather annoyed if they thought that the outcome of their oral examination might depend upon the personal opinion of an individual examiner. If the process was considered to have any validity, then one might reasonably assume that any examiners would arrive at the same conclusions about a dissertation. In other words, that the outcome would not depend upon the personal idiosyncrasies of the examiners. Candidates and their supervisors would, we might assume, want the assessment process to be as consistent as is reasonably possible. A good dissertation would consistently be regarded as good, irrespective of the examiners, and a weak dissertation would consistently be regarded as weak. Kiley and Mullins (2005), however, raise a very interesting dimension of this issue. They have been investigating the process whereby examiners assess research dissertations. In earlier research, it transpired that experienced doctoral examiners did not generally feel it was a good idea to submit dissertations to inexperienced examiners. They particularly felt this was true when the dissertation was generally regarded as being of poor quality. If in fact it were true that there were significant differences in approach between experienced and inexperienced examiners, then it raises a number of important questions. What kind of training takes place for doctoral examiners, in order to try to achieve consistency between institutions? Are experienced examiners more liberal in their approach to examining than inexperienced examiners? What criteria do examiners employ in order to distinguish between a high standard of thesis, and a low quality thesis?

There are a number of different controversies here. There is the controversy about the way in which the assessment of research degrees is managed by universities. There is the controversy about the way in which academics may differ in their opinions of the same dissertation. Finally, there is the controversy about the possible effect of age and experience on the outcome of dissertation examinations. When writing up their research Kiley and Mullins (2005) included a section entitled 'Previous research in the field', which was in effect the literature review for the article. They started with a clear statement of their views about current research in the field. 'There are strong indications in the research that the selection of examiners is critical in the doctoral experience' (p.122). They continued to examine the work of three writers who suggested criteria for the appointment of research examiners. They then explored research on the actual oral examination procedure and the type of questions asked by experienced and inexperienced examiners. They also reviewed research on the comments written on theses which were being examined. Finally, they also noted some fairly recent research which suggested that experienced examiners tended to consider the dissertation holistically. That is they tended to appreciate that in any dissertation there would be both academically sound areas, and also weaker areas. Experienced examiners tended to balance these against each other, which stopped them concentrating on the weaker points and perhaps taking a more negative view of the dissertation. In this article, therefore, there was an awareness of the sensitivity of the subject matter, and of the controversies with regard to the topic. The literature review set the scene well for the data which was presented later in the article, and gave an initial overview of the general issues.

Summarizing

In their research article published in 2001, Jackson and Tinkler investigate the purposes of the PhD viva. The introduction to the article serves also as the literature review. As we have commented before, a research article is usually fairly short, because of the limitations of the journal, and it is not always possible to have all of the conventional sub-titles.

They note that there is an increased interest in investigating the assessment procedures for the doctorate, and suggest two main factors which are bringing this about. This is an example of the use of summarizing as a technique in a literature review. They point first of all to the generally increased interest in carrying out research on PhD processes, and suggest that it is only natural that this should involve an enquiry into the assessment process in general, and the viva voce in particular. Second, the authors argue that there is an increased tendency for the transparency of processes and procedures in universities. Students expect to be fully informed about all the processes which affect them. Particularly this is so with regard to assessment processes. By summarizing the two main motivational factors in encouraging research on the viva voce process, the authors have provided a useful framework for the foreseeable future.

The authors then move on to discuss the possibility of changing the nature of the viva voce examination. They adopt a similar strategy of summarizing the research on this into two main areas. They first of all point out that there is a call from certain quarters for the British viva to be changed to become more similar to those in the United States or the Netherlands. Second, there is the broad argument that the viva should be completely dispensed with. Again, the use of a summarizing technique gives a structure to the literature review.

The final step in adopting the use of summaries in this article is to consider the impact of international cooperation in the supervision and examination of PhDs. The authors point out that research degrees have become a very significant commodity as students move around the world to study. In addition, when students travel overseas to study for and obtain a doctorate, it is an extremely important element in their career progression. However, the international dimension not only concerns students travelling overseas, but, as Jackson and Tinkler point out, the examination process is likely to become more and more international. Overseas academics may increasingly be asked to take part in the examination of doctoral students in British universities.

Consequently, they will want to be informed of the precise details of the British system, in order that they can carry out their functions as examiners. The authors have thus again adopted a summarizing technique, in order to draw together examples of research under a single heading.

Synthesizing

It is important to be analytic and critical in the way in which you categorize the content of your literature review. Sometimes it is necessary to combine articles or ideas, in order to bring an element of cohesion to the literature review. This bringing together and merging of ideas is not always easy, and demands care. There may sometimes be the temptation to combine ideas which do not necessarily have a great deal in common with each other. Synthesis requires the joining of ideas, so that hopefully, in that process, the reader can have a vision of something rather more than formerly existed as an array of disparate parts. In other words, the synthesis is more than the sum of the parts.

In her study of the ethnographic process, Iversen (2009) concentrated particularly upon the way in which ethnographers manage to terminate their research and then separate themselves from the 'field' and the respondents in it. The very nature of ethnographic research requires the researcher to embed themselves in the social situation they are studying, and to get to know the respondents in detail. Only in this way can they begin to see the world through the eyes of the respondents – almost a prerequisite for any mean-ingful ethnographic research. Iversen makes the point that most discussion of the ethnographic research process concentrates upon the issues of access to the field. This is clearly very important, and there are often many obstacles to the researcher gaining access. Nevertheless, unless the researcher intends to 'go native' and to become a permanent member of the social community being studied, then there must inevitably come a time when the researcher must develop an exit strategy.

The problem, however, is that during the period of research, a relationship of varying degrees of closeness often develops between the researcher and the respondents. The researcher gets to know the respondents closely, often feels a sense of moral obligation to them for helping with the research, and perhaps feels that it is not quite ethical to just walk away one day, with no residual continuing commitment. From the respondents' point of view, they may well have come to rely upon the researcher. They may have gained a great deal from the research project, and may have imagined that it would more or less go on for a very long time. The researcher may have told the respondents about the time scale of the research, but they may nevertheless have assumed it would go on longer. Ultimately they may feel very let down if the researcher simply disappears from their lives. Clearly this is a complex situation, and the researcher as the initiator of the research process has the responsibility for finding a sensitive way to end the research programme.

The process of synthesis

In constructing her literature review, Iversen synthesizes different aspects of the ethnographic process, in order to produce three key issues which suggest the importance of debating the process of leaving the research field. She suggests first of all (p. 10), that the contemporary discussion of reflexivity in research is likely to have an effect upon analyzing the process of ending the research. Reflexivity is the appreciation that the researcher and the process of research affect the respondents, while they in turn affect the researcher. One therefore considers aspects of this mutual influence, particularly at the end of the research, when there is some kind of parting of the ways of researcher and respondent.

Second, Iversen points out that research ethics committees in universities and other institutions are increasingly influential. They are increasingly making prescriptions about the ethical considerations which should be taken into account during the research process. One of the main ethical principles in research is that of informed consent. The respondent should be made aware of all the salient features of the research project before they give their consent to take part. One of these features should be the duration of the project, and the timing and process for ending the research. This process should also be such as to not cause any harm or distress to the respondents. All of this should be made perfectly evident before the respondent finally decides to take part. In short, then, it is suggested that the influence of research review boards is such as to require researchers to plan carefully for the end of the research process.

Third, and probably in some ways related to the second point, Iversen points out that there is extensive discussion at the moment about ethnographic methods, and out of this debate will probably naturally arise a consideration of the end process of an ethnographic project. This synthesis of ideas provides a useful means of structuring the literature discussion.

Analyzing

The conduct of a literature review can sometimes provide us with an entirely new dimension upon research into an issue or problem. Many of the major themes for research in education and the social sciences have been investigated in different ways time and time again, and yet the same basic perspective has been used. There is often not the motivation or insight to look completely differently at a research topic. Yet a literature review, if employed creatively, can help us to do just this. An example is research by Kelly, White, Martin and Rouncefield (2006) into the nature of leadership, and particularly leadership within the Further Education sector.

The researchers argue in their introduction and discussion of the literature, that leadership has often been investigated from the point of view of the exceptional skills and qualities of the leader. The leader is perceived as someone with unusual skills in terms of motivating people or inspiring employees. These qualities, which are usually described in terms of being different to those possessed by 'ordinary' people, are very often integrated into a theory of leadership. Such theories give us a means of measuring someone's leadership ability, or of predicting when someone might be an effective leader. The researchers point out, however, that theories of leadership can only help us understand the phenomenon in a very limited way. They argue that the qualities referred to in these theories exist prior to the practical demonstration of leadership. What is important they suggest is the manifestation of leadership in very practical, everyday situations. If we want to understand leadership, and other similar constructs, we should concentrate on exploring the way in which the concept shows itself in ordinary situations such as talking to colleagues, chairing a meeting, or organizing students.

The process of analysis

In order to understand a concept such as leadership in this way, we need to analyze the behaviour of people who are commonly perceived as leaders. After all, 'leaders' probably, one assumes, carry out many of the kinds of activities carried out by 'ordinary' people, although it is at least possible that they carry them out in a different way. They will, for example, read documents, make notes, hold conversations, evaluate problems, keep records of costs, give presentations, and attend or chair meetings. In other words, on one level of understanding, leaders do most of the sorts of things that other employees do. It may be of course, that although they do the same kinds of things, those activities are more 'important', or involve larger sums of money, or involve more confidential matters. In other words, the leadership element lies in the nature of the tasks rather than in the way they are handled by the 'leader'. The other perspective on this is that both leaders and other employees carry out the same types of actions, but the leader carries them out in a qualitatively different manner. In other words, the leader chairs a meeting in a more dynamic, insightful fashion; or the leader has the capacity to make rather more strategic, far-reaching decisions than the 'ordinary' employee.

However, whatever the truth of the matter, the researchers, in their analysis of the literature and of the concept 'leadership', propose that the only way to resolve the issue of the nature of leadership, is to collect empirical data, through ethnographic studies, to reveal something of the ordinary lives of leaders. From an analysis of this data will emerge the characteristics of leadership. These characteristics will not be derived from theories, or grand schema, but will be generated through analysis of ordinary life situations. Such an approach is very much in the tradition of interpretive research, where researchers try not to impose their own structures or understandings on the research field, but to let their analysis emerge from observations of real, everyday events.

Themes

A good journal article will not only report on some research, but will try to draw out a significant issue or theme, which has perhaps a broader relevance than the research topic of the article. Such themes are important for your literature review since they enable you, if need be, to write about broader issues, and to establish links with other articles in your review. In her article on the way in which action research is employed in education, Kinsler (2010) argues that to some extent action research has developed into just another research method to be employed in teacher training, or to try to improve the quality of teaching in schools. The article argues that the emancipatory element of action research is fundamental to the approach, whatever the particular type or context of action research being implemented. In other words, whatever type of action research we are discussing, there should be an underlying purpose of liberating people, of encouraging freedom and autonomy, of enabling people to critique the society in which they live, and to work towards a more participatory and democratic form of living. These features, it is argued, are an indispensable characteristic of action research.

This is an important insight, since it points to what we might regard as universal aspirations of human beings, and indeed what we might think of as the purpose of all research. We might feel that if research of any kind is to have meaning at all, then it should be motivated by the desire to improve the human condition. Hence, if using this particular article in a literature review, it would be very useful to be able to take this theme of emancipation, and weave it into a discussion of the nature of the ultimate purpose of research.

Evaluating

When we evaluate the literature in a literature review we do far more than simply describe it. We may reflect upon the research design, and how well this was planned. We might consider the data collection process and evaluate any potential limitations of the way it was carried out. On the other hand, we might also evaluate the literature in terms of how it helps us understand the subject. Sometimes a research subject is very complex, and if we are an external researcher without any direct experience of the context, it may be difficult for us to truly empathize with the respondents. We may remain an outsider, who goes through the process of collecting data, but who does not fully and completely understand its significance.

McGibbon, Peter and Gallop (2010) carried out an ethnographic study of nurses' stress. This is an area where someone unfamiliar with the context of nursing might have difficulty in understanding the nature of the occupational stress. Even a nurse working in one specialism might not appreciate the stress generated in a different nursing context. The authors, however, all with experience of nursing, produced in their article a very detailed literature review which reveals so much of the potential stress created by the nursing context. By examining the literature on nursing stress, they have evaluated the different types of stress and the kinds of traumatic incidents with which nurses have to cope. To read their literature review is to be deeply moved by the experiences which nurses have to undergo. Their evaluation of the subject of nursing stress helps one to appreciate that when a nurse is helping a patient who has undergone a very traumatic situation, or has suffered a great deal, then in a sense the nurse herself or himself, has to cope with that experience at second hand. For the reader of this article, the literature review opens up a new world of meaning and understanding or the lives of nurses.

Comparing different views on a subject

Research methods as a subject discipline have always been in a state of evolution since they first emerged as an area of study in their own right. This has been particularly so in relation to the use of technology in the collection and analysis of data. A major change has taken place, for example, in the use of computer packages such as SPSS for the analysis of quantitative data. Formerly students and researchers needed to manipulate complex formulae in order to use statistical tests in their data analysis. Statistical packages such as SPSS are very easy to use in terms of entering the data, and obtaining results, but there is an inherent problem. Before the advent of such packages, students needed to follow a detailed course in statistics, in order first of all to appreciate which statistical tests were appropriate for a certain type of data, and then to be able to perform the complex calculations. Finally, when they had calculated their results, they needed to be able to interpret their findings.

Unfortunately, many students do not appreciate that it is still necessary to understand which statistical test to use, and to be able to interpret the results. SPSS will take away the burden of performing the calculations, but the other issues remain. Some academics feel that to some extent the use of statistical packages is resulting in a false sense of security among students. One might even argue that the ready availability of statistical software is encouraging a form of de-skilling in students, who would otherwise have to make an effort to understand statistical analysis.

The process of comparison

The issue of the use of new technology is also having an effect upon qualitative data analysis. Murthy (2008) has written an interesting article on the use of new technologies with regard to collecting digital, ethnographic data. In his review of some of the relevant literature, he has pointed out an apparent reluctance among some writers to discuss the relevance of new technologies for data collection. There may well be differences of opinion here, related to a reluctance to abandon established methods. At any rate, in situations such as this, where innovations in technology result in new ways of approaching research, it is very useful to compare contrasting opinions, since this often enables us to focus on the central concerns and issues of a research perspective.

Taking notes

With the expansion of interest in qualitative research methods and field research has come a much greater use of field diaries and field notes. The idea of note taking as a serious activity has spread. Indeed, the notes themselves are sometimes used as actual data to be analysed reflexively later by the researcher. For field notes to be valuable sources of data, they have to be written in an analytic way, so that there are real insights which can be reflected upon later. The same approach is true for notes taken on the literature for a literature review. You need to always think very analytically, and make notes which interconnect the literature, writing in such a way that there is plenty of material for later discussion and reflection.

Key questions

1 If research is a rational, logical process, why is it that researchers find points of disagreement with each other?
2 In analyzing research articles, why is it important to think carefully about the effects of reflexivity?
3 Why are research ethics committees so important for researchers?

Key reading

Cottrell, S. (2005) *Critical Thinking Skills: Developing Effective Analysis and Argument.* Basingstoke: Palgrave Macmillan.

Gillett, A., Hammond, A. and Martala, M. (2009) *Successful Academic Writing.* Harlow: Pearson Longman.

Judge, B., Jones, P. and McCreery, E. (2009) *Critical Thinking Skills for Education Students.* Exeter: Learning Matters.

Thomson, A. (2009) *Critical Reasoning: A Practical Introduction,* 3rd edn. London: Routledge.

Van den Brink-Budgen, R. (2010) *Critical Thinking for Students: Learn the Skills of Analyzing, Evaluating, and Producing Arguments,* 4th edn. Oxford: How to Books.

6

The structure of a literature review

Summary • Learning outcomes • Subdivisions according to criteria • Headings and sub-headings • Theoretical perspectives used • Type of methodology • Findings • Chronology • Ideological position • Selection of significant works • Key terms • Key questions • Key reading

Summary

Although a dissertation or journal article is normally structured according to fairly widely accepted conventions, there is still considerable room for individual style and creativity when it comes to the plan and structure of the writing and layout. The same is very much true of the literature review. You can select certain elements such as ideology, methodology, or theoretical perspective to have a predominant position in the review chapter, and hence to influence the structure. On the other hand, you can vary the headings and sub-headings to create different structures. In short, to some extent you can use your imagination to create an interesting and stimulating literature review, which enhances the dissertation.

Learning outcomes

After reading this chapter you should be able to do the following:

- Assess the different ways in which your literature review could be structured.
- Compare the advantages and disadvantages of these structures.
- Relate these structures to actual examples from research literature.

Subdivisions according to criteria

It is very important that a literature review has a coherent structure which links with the other elements of the dissertation. It helps if that coherence is reflected in the different sections and sub-sections of the review, and that those sub-sections are selected according to specific criteria. The review then becomes more straightforward, and easier to understand for the reader. This is so, even if the subject is complex with a range of fairly complicated concepts.

An example is an article written by Maginn (2007) on the subject of the use of applied ethnography and collaborative planning in enabling more effective community participation in urban regeneration. The first section of the article is an 'Introduction' (p. 25) in which there is a discussion of the nature of community participation and the potential problems that this can bring in an urban regeneration setting. It is argued that if the local community does not have a full commitment to the redevelopment, then this can result in misunderstandings, alienation and a dysfunctional approach to the regeneration project. In the next sub-section, 'Community, participation and partnerships' (p. 27), it is noted that these terms tend to give the impression of a community with a positive attitude towards democratic decision-making. However, it is argued that this is an assumption which is not necessarily true. In fact, such communities may be constantly changing in composition and in attitudes, and may frequently alter their approach to engaging with regeneration projects.

In the next section, entitled 'Entering neighbourhoods with blinkered vision' (p. 28), it is argued that conflict does not necessarily arise simply between the community and the organization or agency which is organizing the regeneration. The tensions can also occur within the community itself, where different sections may have a different perception of the project which is planned. The next section is entitled 'Collaborative planning' (p. 30) and includes a discussion of the theoretical basis of the concept, along with an evaluation of the way in which ideally it can involve all the different parties to the project working together. A further section entitled 'Ethnography and applied ethnography' (p. 32) examines the notion of applied ethnography, suggesting that it is in effect the traditional concept of ethnography, although trying to draw out the potential for making policy transformations. Overall, this is a conceptually complex subject, and yet the use of clear sections with each devoted to a particular concept or group of related concepts, helps the reader to understand the key arguments which are being proposed.

Some academic writers, while still adhering to the principle of clear structure and sub-divisions, opt for a rather different way of presenting their literature. Dickson-Swift et al. (2007) have written about the nature of doing qualitative research from the point of view of the researcher. In particular, they have researched and discussed the effects of being a qualitative researcher when investigating issues which may be sensitive in one way or another. They note that there has been in the past considerable discussion of the need to take into account the feelings of respondents in qualitative research, but that this study tries to explore the research process from the point of view of the researchers. The article starts with an 'Introduction' section (p. 327) which examines some aspects of the issue, and cites relevant research. There follows a discussion on 'Method' (p. 329) which, among other things, explores the grounded theory perspective. Subsequently, however, instead of a pure literature review, considering only or primarily previous research studies, there are sub-divisions of some of the main themes of the research, in which there are linked discussions of both data from the research and previous literature. The first such section, for example, considers the issue of 'Entering the lives of others' (p. 330). This is a characteristic feature of much qualitative research, and this sub-section discusses the complexities of the issue. As researchers we try to understand the world from the respondents' point of view, and this involves trying to find out about their lives in a very detailed, and often intimate manner. We often become privy to elements of their private lives which other people, even close friends, would not know about. Sometimes, the data obtained may involve aspects of the respondents' lives which have caused them anxiety or worry, and listening to such reports may have adverse effects for the researcher. The sub-section not only cites previous literature on this theme, but also provides data from the actual research study.

The next section on 'Developing rapport' (p. 331) continues this strategy for structuring the literature review. It deals with the complex question of the manner in which researchers establish a relationship with respondents. It notes that researchers do need to establish a certain level of rapport, since only in this way will they be able to encourage the respondents to provide data on their lives. Researchers cannot simply enter someone's life, and collect the data, without inevitably becoming involved to some extent, and this can impose pressures upon the researcher. In addition it seems evident that in many cases respondents can gain an enormous amount from being able to talk about their experiences, even if painful. Having someone to talk to can be very helpful for them, but the process of listening to extensive and intimate disclosures may not be easy for the researcher.

A feature of such research for those carrying it out, is that from time to time they may feel that it is appropriate to mention some features of their own experiences. This may particularly be the case where they have experiences which are close to or particularly relevant to those of the respondents. This issue is dealt with in the next section on 'Self-disclosure' (p. 332). Again there are extracts from the research study, and also citations. This is a difficult issue because, for some researchers, the idea of providing data and comments based upon their own lives may seem to step outside their perceived role as a researcher. On the other hand, some researchers may feel that if they provide comments on their experiences, it may make it much easier for the respondents to talk about their own lives. In a sense, as was noted, this can help to equalize the relationship between the researcher and the respondent.

Overall, then, this approach of using sub-divisions based upon key themes in the reseach, yet linking together citations with research data from the study, may be useful. In a conventional structure for a dissertation, the previous literature and the data from the study are more clearly separated. This then necessitates that you, as the writer, make an effort to keep linking the two together, so that the data from the research is seen as being connected to previous research. With the strategy employed in this article, however, there is a closer link between data and previous research, and this may help when dealing with certain types of research topic.

Headings and sub-headings

The sub-division and structuring of a literature review are very important elements since the structure enables the reader to absorb the information much more easily when reading it, and indeed it also helps the writer or researcher to structure their own thoughts more effectively. The use of sub-headings is an important part of this process, but there is a multiplicity of different ways in which headings are used in practice. They may be used to provide a detailed categorization of features of the literature, or on a more straightforward level to provide a sequence to the account. The latter is probably typical of the article by Vongkhamphra, Davis and Adem (2010), which details the process of the resettlement of an African refugee family in the United States.

The article starts with a historical account of the Bantu people in south-central Africa, and their original displacement to Somalia through the slave trade. It explains the tragedy which afflicted them during the Somali civil war of recent times, and their attempts to find a new home nearer to their countries of origin. It then explains the efforts of the United Nations High Commissioner for Refugees to negotiate with the US government to accept a number of Bantu refugees for resettlement in America. The next section of the article, entitled 'Refugee resettlement in the USA' (p. 248) explains the overall process through which new refugees are guided. In particular, this section of the article explains the nature and work of the 'voluntary resettlement agencies'. These are the actual organizations which put in place the detailed systems for caring for resettled refugees. The next section of the article, 'The resettlement agency' (p. 249) examines in detail the functioning of each agency, and the time scale within which they would normally hope to help a refugee become independent in the United States. The following sections of the article deal with the case study which forms the basis of the article. The case study concerns a mother and her five children who are resettled in the United States. The next main section is entitled 'Case study', and is followed by sub-sections which are entitled 'First month' and 'Second month', which detail the gradual process of resettlement, and the orientation process by which the family gradually adjusts to life in their new country. The article concludes with sections which summarize the results of the process for the case study family and also for the resettlement agency. The concluding section of the article entitled 'Discussion' (p. 255) tries to draw together some general themes from the resettlement experience of the case study family, including noting the often very traumatic experiences undergone by refugee families before their resettlement in a new country. Overall, this article does not use a great many references, probably because of the nature of the research. The process of detailing the life history of resettlement of one family does perhaps not encourage the use of many citations. Nevertheless, there are a number of citations integrated with the discussions of the history of the Bantu people, and also with the overall resettlement process. In this article, however, the use of headings helps enormously to lead the reader through the complex process of resettlement, and also to enable the researchers to make comments about the resettlement process in general.

Theoretical perspectives used

In many research articles, theoretical discussions form the basis for the sub-divisions and structure of the literature review. In a journal article, where the number of words is often limited by the demands of the journal, there is sometimes insufficient space to have a literature review which concentrates solely upon subject matter. If this were the case, there may not be sufficient space in the article to discuss any data or findings. For this reason, discussion of the literature is often either integrated with other aspects of the article, or presented as part of the debate about theoretical issues. The situation is different in a dissertation, where there is usually much more space, and it is possible to have a literature review which evaluates the previous research on a subject in a broad and detailed way. However, the different approaches outlined in this chapter are used in dissertations, depending very much upon the subject matter of the research.

In an article by Freshwater et al. (2010) the subject matter of the article is in effect, theoretical issues in research, and consequently it is natural to make this the basis of the structure of the article. In addition, the discussion of literature is integrated with the sections devoted to subject matter. The focus of this article is the assertion that in general terms qualitative research is sometimes perceived as not quite as rigorous as quantitative research. The first section of the article entitled 'Background' (p. 498) argues that in broad terms quantitative research is sometimes perceived as having a higher status within the circles of those organizations which dispense funds for research. This, it is suggested, is true within the field of health studies, which is the context of this article. Fundamentally, it is argued, one of the major concerns is with the nature of the evidence which is presented to justify an argument, and sometimes the kind of evidence adduced in quantitative studies is perceived as being perhaps more 'scientific' and 'objective'. Qualitative research, by its nature, tends to have a rather more subjective focus, and to place more emphasis upon an interpretive approach to data, and the exploration of the interaction between research and respondent. It is also suggested that articles which adopt a quantitative approach, with a related approach to the nature of evidence, may be somewhat advantaged in terms of gaining publication in prestigious journals. The article then sets out to discuss two approaches to qualitative research which, it is asserted, may provide the kinds of evidence which could be accepted as comparable to those of quantitative research.

The first approach is that of discourse analysis, and the sub-section is entitled 'Discourse as evidence' (p. 500). The authors argue that within this perspective there is the assumption that there is a relationship between the nature of discourse within a social context, and the way in which power and authority are distributed and demonstrated. In other words, the way in which people speak about, discuss and write about their professional lives and activities, is related to the definitions of power and knowledge within professional organizations. The authors make the interesting point (p. 502) that one of the main purposes of this type of research perspective, is not necessarily to generate findings which are widely applicable, but rather to raise questions about issues in research, so that people can be encouraged to think in different ways about the world.

The next theoretical perspective to be explored is that of auto-ethnography, in a section entitled 'Self as evidence: Auto-ethnographical research' (p. 503). This approach to research attempts to provide an account of the experiences of a person in relation to a particular context or issue. The aim is to produce an account which is sufficiently systematic to enable readers not only to understand and empathize with the **ethnography**, but also to provide a basis upon which the ethnographic account can be systematically analyzed. This section also provides a range of citations to related research. The conclusion to the paper reiterates the aim of trying to show that it should be possible to have approaches in qualitative research which match, in terms of quality criteria, those of traditional quantitative research.

A similar issue is discussed by Torrance (2008). Again, the subject matter of the article is the relationship between qualitative and quantitative research, and hence concerns with this form the basis for the structure of the article.

Like the previous article, citations are embedded in the discussion of theoretical issues, and in a sense, one might argue that there is not a separate literature review for the whole article.

The article commences with the suggestion that there is a developing movement which tends to favour the use of traditional 'scientific' experimental methods in educational research, and in particular randomized controlled trials (p. 507). The critics of qualitative studies sometimes suggest that these are often too localized to form the basis for major policy decisions, and that there should be more of an emphasis upon well-designed quantitative research. The next main section of the article examines randomized controlled trials (RCTs) and is entitled 'The Case For and Against RCTs' (p. 509). This section contains a large number of citations, and is in effect a small-scale literature review. The next section is on the topic of 'The Response of Qualitative Research' (p. 513) and discusses, among other things, the movement to try to develop central criteria by which qualitative research can be judged. If there existed a set of such criteria which were generally accepted by qualitative researchers, then, it is supposed, this might go some way to inspiring confidence in qualitative research. Subsequent sections deal with the way such issues are being addressed in the United Kingdom, and then in the United States. The next section is entitled 'Toward a Different Approach' (p. 520) and suggests (p. 521) that the very nature of qualitative research, may make it rather problematic to try to delineate a precise set of criteria or standards by which it may be judged. This article has an extensive list of references, and these are mentioned and discussed throughout the article. One could therefore view the article as in a sense having a series of literature reviews, as each aspect of the overall theoretical issue is addressed. This method is not unknown in dissertations, where some students, in conjunction with their supervisors, may feel that a single, large-scale literature review is inappropriate, and a series of subject-based chapters with citations might be better. To some extent, decisions such as this depend upon the nature and subject matter of the individual research study.

Theoretical perspective as a general form of structure

One way in which we can use theory to structure a literature review is to consider our general view of the world. It is possible, for example, to think of the world as essentially measurable. This can be related to the physical world, where we measure, say, the electrical resistance of a wire, or the phosphorus content of the soil. However, the advocates of this type of approach also apply it to the social world. Social scientists who adopt this perspective consider it possible to measure, say, attitudes, or the degree of integration of a community, or the exercise of power and authority. These approaches often tend to lead to quantitative methods of collecting data.

> On the other hand, a different world view is represented by those who feel that the world is essentially unmeasurable. They feel that human behaviour and human relationships are so complex that to try to measure them is ultimately flawed. According to them, human interaction can be described, it can be compared between one person and another, it can be evaluated and analysed, but it cannot be measured. Such an approach is likely to lead to forms of qualitative data collection.
>
> These two broad categories could be used as a means of categorizing research literature, and dividing it into sections for a literature review.

Type of methodology

Methodological issues are central to the research process, and as such, often constitute one of the main ways in which a literature review can be structured. If there is a conventional way in which to structure a dissertation, it is to preserve the literature on the subject matter of the dissertation in the literature review chapter, and then to address the literature on methodology in a separate chapter devoted to research design, data collection and analysis. However, it does happen that the methodological issues are sometimes a central element of the subject matter of the study, and hence the literature on method is analysed within the main literature review. Alternatively, the literature on method may be fully integrated throughout the early chapters of the dissertation. The example of research writing to be considered next has methodology at the very heart of the subject matter. Indeed, like the discussions in the previous section, this article is in a sense concerned with the quality of qualitative research, although it addresses this issue in a fundamental way by reflecting upon the very nature of research. The article by Carter and Little (2007) considers the movement to evaluate qualitative research by means of a checklist which in principle could be applied to any example of qualitative research. However, they circumvent the issue of checklists as a means of assessing quality in research, and return to the basics of the research process by a careful and thorough analysis of the three terms of epistemology, methodology and method. The article is devoted throughout to a discussion of these three concepts, and uses an extensive range of sub-headings to provide structure for the article. Citations are integrated throughout, and hence the article consists in a sense of an analysis of subject-matter combined with an evaluation of literature.

The article begins with a brief introduction which outlines the problem to be addressed. The authors note the ongoing debate about the best means of evaluating qualitative research, and in particular of determining its quality. The next section of the article is one in which there is an attempt to clarify the concepts of epistemology, methodology and method. The authors point out that in the writing on research these terms are very often used in different ways, and indeed defined in different ways (p. 1317). This is a very important point, and I feel sure that many, many students have been confused by the way in which these basic terms are given so many different nuances by writers. These are some of the fundamental concepts of the discipline of research, and it is very difficult to write about research if there is no shared agreement about the nature of such concepts. Indeed, this problem is exacerbated when trying to structure a literature review around key ideas in methodology, when there does not appear to be a standard way of using the ideas. The authors try to rectify this problem by providing very clearly expressed statements about these concepts, and by including citations to a range of writers to support and illustrate their contentions. In some cases the writers employ more than one brief definition of a term, to illustrate the slightly different approach taken by writers. These quotations are carefully selected so that they do not confuse the reader, but illustrate the alternative ways in which writers choose to write about concepts. Nevertheless, the writers of the present article manage to draw out from these quotations sufficient commonality to leave us with a clear understanding of how they are interpreting and using these three important concepts.

Over the years, generations of teachers must have given a significant piece of advice to their students in many different subjects. When starting an essay or a piece of work, always begin by 'defining your terms'! When I was at school, I know many of my teachers said this to me over and over again! It remains one of the best pieces of advice a teacher can give. Yet it is rather strange that in a subject area like social science research, which should be an area of rational, logical enquiry *par excellence*, university academics can use basic concepts in apparently different ways. The present writers make the point (p. 1318) that the concept 'methodology' is not used in a consistent way, and I feel sure that I am guilty of this myself. They point out that the term is often employed almost as a synonym for a social science perspective such as ethnography, or for an approach more closely linked to actual data collection, such as participant observation. On the other hand, they point out that the term can also be used to indicate the discipline of analyzing and reflecting upon the methods used in research. The present writers thus articulate two very different ways of using the concept 'methodology'.

Considering for a moment the use of the term methodology to designate a type of research perspective, the writers then list some of the many different perspectives which are often embraced under the term qualitative research. In addition, they list some of the key writers who are usually associated with each perspective. It is important for the reader to be aware of such key writers, at least partly so that they can look up references and familiarize themselves with the perspective on a deeper level. However, the citing of writers of so-called **seminal works** does pose some problems for the student writing a literature review. If a writer is very well known in a particular field, it is easy for you to wonder whether you should mention them. You may well think that the external examiner for your dissertation will consider such writers to be so well known that it is unnecessarily obvious to mention their names. I would argue that it is definitely worth mentioning them in a literature review, on the grounds that to omit them would make the review incomplete. On the other hand, it may not be necessary to discuss each seminal work in detail, since to do so would take up valuable space perhaps better devoted to more recent, specialized research which may be more specifically connected with your own work. The writers of this article employ sub-headings extensively to structure the discussion. For example, they start with 'Definitions and Explanations' (p. 1317) followed by 'Epistemology: Justifying Knowledge', 'Methodology: Justifying Method', and 'Method: Research Action'. One of the advantages of using a very detailed structure of sub-headings in this case, is that this is a philosophically complex issue, and by presenting the arguments in a systematic and logical fashion, they are easier for the reader to understand.

The next sub-heading is entitled 'The Need to Reconsider These Basic Principles' (p. 1319), and addresses some of the reasons for this debate being important. One of the reasons given is that of 'methodological fundamentalism' (p. 1319). Some researchers appear to form the value judgement that a particular qualitative research approach can make the best contribution to social science enquiry. They become extremely committed to one form of qualitative research, and appear to advocate it whatever the particular research problem being addressed, or the research context. In that case, their favoured qualitative approach becomes a form of research ideology. When this happens, there is a danger that the research approach will become self-defining as of high quality, and incorporating a high level of rigour. The researcher concerned may begin to feel that no further assessment of quality is necessary. The research is self-referentially of a high standard. One should always guard against making explicit or implicit assumptions like this in a literature review. A valid analysis of literature should be open-minded and sceptical, and should apply clear criteria to the assessment of research reports and writing. This is one of the reasons for the advocacy of the use of these three terms, epistemology, methodology and method. They provide clear standards of judgement, yet standards which are sufficiently flexible to apply to the many different forms of qualitative research which are available.

On the other hand, although a balanced objectivity in both research and in writing a literature review may appear desirable goals, it is worth considering whether value judgements are in fact inseparable from research. If we consider, for example, the choice of a research topic, this is based upon the decision that this issue or problem is worth investigating. That decision inevitably attaches primacy to one research issue at the expense of others. The reasons for attaching that significance to one research question, and not to another, may be diverse and numerous. Every student, researcher or academic has had a different education. They have read perhaps some of the same books, but also different books. They have all interacted in different ways with the knowledge which has been presented to them, and as a result of these and many other factors, they interpret and analyze the world in different ways. Therefore when selecting a research question we are influenced by these kinds of factors.

Carter and Little (2007) point out that the type of epistemology favoured by an individual may be at least partly influenced by the broad subject area in which the researcher or student has been educated (p. 1325). For example, if a student has studied sociology at Bachelor and Master degree levels, and particularly if these courses were taught by lecturers heavily influenced by interpretive sociology, then this is likely to affect the way such a student formulates a research question. The student will probably be interested in investigating the perceptions of a small sample of people, and will try to avoid influencing the research design too much themselves. Indeed there may not even be anything substantive which could be called a research design. On the other hand, if a student has studied under lecturers who tended to prefer a broader, large-scale investigation, and who were influenced primarily by a positivist epistemology, then this is likely to influence the student. They may well reflect this type of epistemology in the design of their own research.

Whatever type of epistemology is selected by an individual does reflect the education and background of a researcher or student, and is to an extent, based upon their values and norms. In addition, as stressed by the present writer, the epistemological decisions do affect the methodology and method. An interpretive epistemology implies a certain kind of methodology such as ethnomethodology or phenomenology. In turn, these then suggest a particular type of method, or data collection strategy. Now these three concepts, whichever are chosen, will have an effect upon the types of literature selected for the review, and indeed for the way in which that literature is analysed. A positivist will select certain types of literature, and will then look for certain types of quality in it. An interpretivist will also select literature which reflects that particular epistemological approach, and will also analyze the literature from their own perspective. Both of these approaches could yield research studies of the highest quality, depending on the way in which the data is collected and analyzed. The particular epistemology, methodology and method will also affect the kinds of sub-headings used in the literature review and the way in which the student or researcher seeks to organize the material.

The type of method used to collect and analyze data is also sometimes employed as a means of structuring a literature review. For example, if a **mixed method** approach is used in a dissertation, then part of the data may be collected by means of a questionnaire, and part using semi-structured interviews. The researcher may assemble some examples of research which use questionnaires, and other examples which use interviews. These could be used as the basis for subdivisions in the literature review. There are other ways in which the method of the research may be used as a structural basis for the literature review. There are many different types of sampling strategy in use in research, and it may be possible to identify a range of literature which all employ the same sampling method. In interpretive research where we may broadly refer to purposive sampling, there are many different ways in which a purposive sample may be put together. These could form the basis for a section of a literature review.

Although this article has as its principal purpose to design a basic conceptual structure whereby it might be possible to judge the quality of a wide range of types of qualitative research, it also can be adapted to provide strategies for structuring a literature review. Its analysis of epistemology, methodology and method provides a basis for subdividing literature, and hence of structuring a review.

Good practice

With regard to the relative diversity of ways in which some terms may be defined in the social sciences, there are several approaches which you can take to the issue. The first is to select a key writer and to use his or her definition of a term. This should be clearly referenced and you should make it clear that you have selected this definition from a range of alternatives. It would also probably help if you explained the reasons for selecting this particular definition to use throughout your writing.

A second approach would involve discussing and analyzing the various definitions and use of a concept which are commonly found in the literature. You could then select one definition to use in your dissertation and explain the reasons for your selection. This is a comprehensive approach, but could be time-consuming because of the discussion of different interpretations. Finally, you could define the concept yourself, drawing upon examples of usage in the literature, and explaining the reasons for taking this particular perspective. All three of these approaches are acceptable, and the choice you make may depend on the particular circumstances and also the nature of the concept itself.

Findings

In the conventional structure of a dissertation the literature review appears fairly near the beginning, while the data and the findings appear in the second half of the dissertation. However, although this is the standard structure, there are always types of dissertation or research report which introduce variations depending upon the research design involved.

Veltri (2008) presents a long and interesting analysis of the Teach for America (TFA) scheme. This is a project whereby recent college and university graduates in the United States teach for a period of time – often two years – in relatively deprived city areas. The Teach for America scheme has received considerable financial support from major corporations in America. It places often very intelligent, and high performing young graduates in schools where the students can be very challenging, and often come from a different ethnic background to that of the young person teaching them. The introduction to the article provides citations to background literature related to the issues raised by the Teach for America scheme. It also notes the strong sense of idealism which pervades the scheme, and which presumably is attractive to the large business corporations which support it. The journal article reports on a qualitative study which lasted for eight years, and which collected a considerable quantity of data on the day-to-day working of the scheme. The next section of the article is entitled TFA's 'Service' Model (p. 514), and starts with a discussion of the grants made available to participants. The young graduates can use these grants for the payment of higher education fees, and as one young person noted, she intended to use the grants to contribute towards her Masters degree tuition fees (p. 514). It is interesting that here, very early in the article, there is an example of transcribed data from one of the participants. In a conventional research report, this would be in the second half of the report.

It is also noted in this section of the article, that the young people who volunteer for the Teach For America project, are given a short period of teacher training before they actually work in the schools to which they have been allocated. This short teacher training course lasts for five weeks and includes basic classroom skills along with short periods of experience in practical teaching situations. Research evidence is adduced which suggests that a significant number of school principals are impressed with the teaching abilities of TFA graduates. On the other hand, at least one young teacher suggests in data, that the early experiences of the teaching in urban schools were extremely difficult and challenging.

The article now begins to present large quantities of transcribed data, sometimes from interviews and sometimes from field diaries kept by those who provided the teacher training or who mentored the young graduates. The next section (p. 516) is entitled 'Notes from the Field: Unwarranted Visitation'. This section consists entirely of notes transcribed from a field diary, and concerns a visit by a female police officer to one classroom, where she removed student backpacks for examination. From now on in the article, empirical qualitative data predominates in the sub-sections, and indeed on a good many pages the number of lines of data exceeds the number of lines written by the journal article author.

The next section is entitled 'Site-Based Realities: Learning the Community Culture' (p. 517). The extracts of empirical data make compulsive reading as they provide accounts of the events which the TFA recruits have to face. Essentially, many of the young teachers are working in deprived urban areas of which normally they would probably have little or no experience. The students they are teaching experience traumas, difficulties, and sometimes violence on a level which seems completely alien to the more middle-class young teachers who are working with them. Very often, the young teachers do not know how to respond for the best, and have to simply negotiate their way through the situations in which they find themselves. That they usually manage to do this is a great compliment to their youthful enthusiasm for the TFA project, and their determination to do something useful with this period in their lives. The data demonstrates how the teachers slowly begin to understand aspects of the culture of the school and the culture of the catchment area. In many cases the culture to which they were exposed was new and very strange, but sometimes (p. 522) the young teachers found that they possessed skills which made an immediate link with their students. Some of the teachers in one group spoke Spanish and found themselves teaching children whose mother-tongue was Spanish. The children were extremely impressed, and this helped the teachers forge a link with their students. Two more sections in the article provide further data, integrated with references where these are relevant. Nevertheless, the prime focus of these sections was to present transcriptions from the data.

Towards the end of the article, there is a section entitled 'Discussion' (p. 536) which draws together some of the themes which have emerged from the data. However, this section only consists of about two pages of text, and does not address the numerous issues which are brought out in the previous data sections. This is not necessarily a failing in the article, because in some ways the analysis of the data proceeds as the data is gradually revealed throughout the article. This then enables the references and the literature review to be written in parallel with the findings and analysis. The major point made in the Discussion section, however, is the perhaps unpalatable one of equality of opportunity. It argues that behind all the rhetoric of the Teach For America scheme lies a fundamental lack of fairness. It argues that in the affluent areas of the United States there is no need for the TFA scheme, since the schools are staffed with well-qualified, trained and experienced teachers. This does not prevail of course in the poorer, disadvantaged areas, where the children often have teachers who stay for only a very short time, or they are taught by the minimally trained young people of the TFA scheme. Despite the undoubted achievements of the TFA scheme, it is argued that all children should be taught by the kind of teachers who generally work in the affluent areas. Finally, at the end of the article are two short sections, one on the process for collecting and analyzing the data, and one on the sampling procedure. The article thus has an unorthodox structure, but it demonstrates how an interesting and informative article can be constructed around the presentation of data and findings, which are linked to a discussion of relevant literature.

Using findings as the basis of the structure of a review

The standard structure of a research report or dissertation has evolved fundamentally because it is logical and rational, and to that extent reflects an idealized model of the research process itself. However, particularly with the expansion in the use of qualitative methods, researchers have experimented with the use of different ways of collecting and analyzing data. For example, they have used various approaches which involve self-reflection and self-observation, and autobiographical accounts. This experimentation with types of data, which would probably previously have been regarded as rather subjective, has also resulted in newer ways of reporting research. The research process has, among many researchers, ceased to be thought of as a supremely rational, linear process. It is sometimes perceived as less linear in style, and perhaps more like a matrix, with the researcher exploring avenues in the research which later seem to be cul-de-sacs, and then trying new approaches. The research process is seen as involving a good deal of trial and error. This in turn has led to attempts to find different ways of reporting research, which are not structured in quite so conventional a way. This is where the data and findings of a research study might be seen as a useful way of basing the reporting of the research, and of the literature review.

Chronology

Chronology is perhaps one of the most obvious of ways in which a literature review can be structured. Typically by starting with the earliest references which are relevant to the subject matter, you can show something of the development of the subject. Sometimes the earliest works may not be very revealing, simply because the subject was in the early stages of its development. Such early works may not employ the full range of concepts which are today associated with a subject area. The analysis may appear to be rather naïve simply because there was not as much literature at the time, to include in the discussion and evaluation. Finally, the analysis may appear rather 'dated' and unfashionable compared with the ideas which circulate in the contemporary world. However, the chronological approach can achieve a great deal by illustrating the history of ideas in a particular subject, and demonstrating the possible ways in which ideas developed sequentially, each influenced by the previous piece of research. One further advantage of a chronological approach, is that the early writers in a discipline quite often set out to establish some theoretical principles which could have a cohesive function in the subject area. They would often try to provide a theoretical foundation, because this would perhaps establish the subject firmly as a legitimate academic discipline. Such a theoretical base might also provide a foundation upon which later academics could build their own advances. The importance of early theory in a subject area is illustrated by the next article by Bullough, Jr. and Pinnegar (2001). They explore the use of data from autobiographies and self-study as a form of research data. They pose the question of how we can judge this kind of investigation as a form of research, and indeed how we can judge its effectiveness and the extent of its valid contribution to knowledge. In order to think more clearly about these questions, they have returned to one of the major sociologists of the twentieth century, C. Wright Mills. They argue that the theoretical orientation of Mills can help in appreciating how autobiographical studies can form a serious research study.

To put it briefly, Mills argues (pp. 14–15) that the experiences of the individual human being cannot truly be understood without setting them in the historical and social context of society. Equally, on the other hand, we cannot appreciate the larger forces which mould our society, without trying to understand the nature of individual social experience. To expand on that slightly, it is suggested that we are all moulded by the micro social forces which operate between individuals. These forces affect us at an individual level, but they are not the only forces which operate on our lives. Society at the macro level is affected by large-scale economic, political, economic and historical forces which have a collective effect upon the individual. No matter how much we try, we cannot escape the consequences and effects of these major forces. They have consequences for each individual citizen.

We can argue, therefore, that superficial autobiographical research is simply a subjective account of how one person feels at a particular moment. However, in order to give that the status of research, we need to explore the way in which a subjective account is influenced by the broader forces prevalent in society at the time. Hence one can argue that literature arranged in chronological order can sometimes be useful in terms of examining the way in which theoretical perspectives arose in the earlier stages of development of a subject.

Common pitfall

When assuming a chronological approach in reviewing literature, it is important to be aware that in the history of a discipline there can very often be major changes of perspective. These might almost amount to paradigmatic changes. The subject or discipline develops a major new way of looking at the world. This might be through a natural process of evolution of thought, or it might be due to the publications of a radical new thinker. In the early stages of development of sociology, for example, sociologists attempted to measure what they perceived as 'social facts'. They assumed that society could be reduced to concepts and ideas which could be measured, usually quantitatively. There developed later, however, the view that society could not be regarded as fixed and certain, and hence definitively measured. The view developed that society was, in a sense, continually creating itself, or that the people who constituted society were continually creating it. This was a very different way of looking at the social world.

If you do adopt a chronological approach to literature analysis, it is important to try to identify such points of hiatus in historical development, to discuss and analyze them, and to try to account for their existence.

Ideological position

I have suggested at various places in this book that objectivity is, *per se*, a valuable and desirable quality in writing a literature review, and perhaps, by implication, in educational writing in general. If we were to ask a group of teachers and students whether it was possible to think and write objectively, I suspect a good many of them would answer in the affirmative. If then we were to ask them what roughly they meant by objectivity, I suspect they would say something like 'thinking in a balanced way' or 'discussing both sides of an issue'. However, whether it is truly possible to think in a completely balanced way may be debatable. It could be that whenever we start to talk about something or enter into a discussion, we do so, at least slightly, from a preordained viewpoint. Certainly to think ideologically is not objective. The ideologue has a supremely committed point of view, such that she or he does not wish to consider any way of looking at an issue, which is different from their favoured perspective. However, even someone who thinks of themselves as open-minded may commence their analysis of an issue from a personally favoured viewpoint. They may hardly realize they are doing it!

In the next article to be discussed, Apple (2008) makes an interesting assertion. In the introduction (p. 241), he suggests that to be involved in education is to be involved in a political enterprise. This does not signify an involvement in party politics, although that could be part of it. Essentially, he is arguing that to teach or to take part in education in any other way, is to be part of the various choices which have to be made in society, and to in effect support a particular way of organizing and structuring society. For example we can conceive of society as being essentially unfair and unequal, with a dominant class which uses a number of strategies at its disposal to sustain that unequal division of wealth and power in society. In this case, one of the purposes of education would be to challenge that system, to explain to students in school why the system is so unfair, and to try to use the education system to attempt to transform society. On the other hand, we may view society as being basically fair, while acknowledging that some people progress further than others, perhaps through their own intelligence and hard work. Within this view the purpose of education is to sustain the present structure of society, because it is perceived as being essentially fair and functional.

Within the first perspective, educationalists would analyze the education system in order to identify examples of curriculum or pedagogy which seem to sustain inequalities. In the second perspective, educationalists would try to find ways to make the education system more efficient and effective. They would not want to change it in any significant way, but to try to make it function better. In short, then, education is political because it is difficult to separate a consideration of an education system from a consideration of the type of society in which it functions. The fairness or unfairness of society will to some degree be reflected in the education system.

Apple writes from the perspective of inequality in society, and analyses the interaction between political action and attempts to change the education system. The next section of the article entitled 'Remembering real schools and real children' provides anecdotes illustrating inequalities. The titles of subsequent sections, for example, 'The politics of educational reform' and 'Understanding conservative social movements in education' make clear the political nature of the discussion. In fact, one can argue that there is no problem with the politicization of educational debate, because education is inevitably political in nature. However, one might argue that a writer on educational matters should always make clear his or her value position and political orientation, in order to avoid claims that they are being unnecessarily ideological in their writing. As long as they do make clear the perspective within which they are writing, then the reader can incorporate that understanding in the way in which they interpret what is written. Ideological or political perspectives form a useful way of structuring a literature review, because they usually incorporate fundamental concepts such as equality, justice, fairness, meritocracy, goodness, liberty and freedom. Since these are such basic concepts they often form an ideal way in which literature can be structured and discussed.

Selection of significant works

The final way to be considered for the structure of a review is through the key works of a single author or perhaps the principal works of a subject area. In many ways, these provide a very straightforward way of structuring a literature review. In the case of the principal works of an author, these can be considered one by one, and integrated with discussion about other examples of literature on the same topic. An example of this approach is the article by Costa (2006) in which she analyses the writings of the political scientist, William Galston. She examines such concepts as civic education, liberalism, liberal democracy, and pluralism in the writing of Galston, citing from his works, and incorporating this analysis with a discussion of other writers in the area. Classification of the literature review into sections becomes relatively easy, based upon the principal works of the author being considered.

The other approach is to consider significant works, not of a single author, but connected to a particular field of study. This provides again a straightforward way in which to structure a literature review. An example would be the article by Cho and Trent (2006) on the subject of validity in qualitative research. The article contains detailed citations on relevant literature, and is divided up into sections on different aspects of validity, such as 'Two general approaches to validity' (p. 321) and 'Transactional validity' (p. 322). In using this technique you need to first of all identify as much of the key literature in the field as possible, and then to divide it up into categories, which will function as the basis of the different sub-divisions. The process may take a little time, but is relatively uncomplicated to put into practice.

We thus reach the end of our discussion of ways to structure a literature review. From our analysis of a range of literature reviews in academic journal articles, we can see that academics employ a range of techniques. This points to the creative nature of much academic writing. The way in which scholarly writing is presented depends very much upon the subject matter, and other issues such as the methodology used. Although we can sketch out some basic principles, an academic writer also needs to be flexible, and to try to think of the most appropriate ways in which to treat a subject.

Key terms

Ethnography: a qualitative research methodology, which places great emphasis on trying to reveal and understand the way respondents look at the world. It is often associated with the use of participant observation.

Mixed method: a type of research design which incorporates two or more different types of research methods, often one quantitative and one qualitative. The use of different methods may be a form of methodological triangulation, and increase validity to some extent.

Seminal work: a book or published research study which has become famous, either because it has broken new ground in a subject area, or perhaps was one of the earlier, founding studies in a subject.

Key questions

1 When we are conducting interpretive or ethnographic research, and need to establish a relationship or empathy with respondents, what issues should we bear in mind?
2 What are the advantages in having sub-headings in a literature review?
3 For what reasons is qualitative research often not regarded as rigorous as quantitative research?

Key reading

Denscombe, M. (2010) *The Good Research Guide: For Small-Scale Social Research Projects*, 4th edn. Maidenhead: Open University Press.

Kamler, B. and Thomson, P. (2006) *Helping Doctoral Students Write: Pedagogies for Supervision*. Abingdon: Routledge.

Murray, R. (2011) *How to Write a Thesis*, 3rd edn. Maidenhead: Open University Press.

Phillips, E. and Pugh, D.S. (2010) *How to Get a PhD*, 5th edn. Maidenhead: Open University Press.

Thomas, G. (2007) *Education and Theory: Strangers in Paradigms*. Maidenhead: Open University Press.

7

Writing the review

Summary • Learning outcomes • Placing themes in order • Compare literature which reaches different conclusions • Being critical of inadequacies • Prose style • Standard approaches to referencing • Citing electronic sources • Calculating the number of quotations to include • Devote more space to discussing significant literature • Key terms • Key questions • Key reading

Summary

An academic dissertation represents a particular genre of writing. Just as a poem, a play, a novel or a biography each demand a specific writing style, so does an academic article or dissertation. They are all creative activities, to the degree that all writing is creative. All writing has as its fundamental aim the process of communication with a reader. The writing of a literature review, as an element of the writing of a dissertation, demands its own set of skills. This chapter examines the actual process of writing a literature review, and the skills which are required. It looks at some of the planning which is required just before the writing begins, and also such features as the prose style, and the use of references and quotations.

Learning outcomes

After reading this chapter you should be able to do the following:

- Select an appropriate prose style for the literature review.
- Insert references and quotations in your review in an acceptable style.
- Select and refer to electronic source material in an appropriate style.

Placing themes in order

The task of actually writing the literature review raises a number of practical questions, notably concerning the order in which the different aspects of the literature will be treated. There are usually a variety of different options available. The order which you select depends a great deal upon the subject matter of the research, and also upon your own viewpoint. One of the best guides in selecting the order for writing a literature review is to read the way others have approached the issue. Although no two situations are the same, it does help to provide ideas.

Czymoniewicz-Klippel et al. (2010) discussed the difficulties and issues in ensuring sound ethics procedures when conducting research. However, instead of concentrating on research ethics procedures in a 'Western' context, they examined the problems when conducting research with people in developing countries. In particular, they wanted to explore the issue of collecting data from 'vulnerable' people – or those who, for a variety of reasons, may find difficulty in appreciating the nature of the research project, and the role which they were being invited to adopt within it. The writers also selected for particular attention a specific aspect of research ethics, that of informed consent. In broad terms, this is the principle that before agreeing to take part in a research study as a respondent, people should have as complete an understanding of the research as possible, and what they will be expected to do. Only in this way is their acquiescence really meaningful. It is therefore necessary for the researchers to give careful thought to the way in which they will provide information about the research for potential respondents.

They start the discussion of their research by commenting upon the way in which research ethics committees operate in giving approval for research to be carried out. They note that a tradition has developed in Western countries whereby the ethics committee has a checklist of issues which are used to monitor proposed research. The system can thus become rather formal, and may not be suited to the situation in a developing country. While still retaining the essential values of research ethics procedures, it may be necessary to adapt these processes to the very different cultural situations in some developing countries. The research article examines the particular ethical issues in research being conducted in India, Papua New Guinea, and Cambodia. In particular, the research examines the ethical issues involved in assuring **informed consent** in situations where data is being collected in these countries.

The next section of the article looks at issues specifically concerned with informed consent. The section is termed 'Informed Consent: Strategies and Strictures' (p. 333) and raises a number of interesting and complex issues. First of all, it notes the current practice in Western countries of asking participants to sign a consent form agreeing to participate in the research. In addition, participants are usually given a fairly detailed summary of the research. This can sometimes be written in language which is not entirely comprehensible to the proposed participants. However much researchers try to write their research summaries in straightforward language, sometimes potential participants do not understand them. It is evident that when working and researching in an entirely different culture with a different language, that helping people to understand the purpose of the research will be difficult. The writers also point out that it can be argued that this approach of obtaining consent signatures, is designed first and foremost to protect the researchers and the institution which is sponsoring their research. The system then, it can be argued, has a kind of legal function rather than primarily trying to protect the welfare of the research participants. The authors have referred to extensive literature to support and illustrate their arguments. They note that some writers feel that the principal responsibility of researchers is to demonstrate care for respondents, and that this is particularly so in the case of respondents who might be judged to be vulnerable in various ways. The manner in which the article authors treat their literature review is very rational, moving through a series of general, more theoretical issues, before starting to examine issues which arise from the case studies of developing countries.

Compare literature which reaches different conclusions

One of the key features of academic writing is that it tends to be understated in style. If one academic completely disagreed with another, and indeed thought the other was completely and utterly wrong about something, he or she would probably say they were in the process of reconciling minor differences of opinion! It is true that some academics can be forthright and outspoken, but as a general rule they tone down very much what they say. It is important therefore when we hear academics say that they have slight reservations about something, they may well mean that they completely disagree with it! This style therefore represents something of the culture which is prevalent in the academic world, and is certainly present in the general way in which literature reviews are written. The style is influenced by an assumption that it is difficult to know something with certainty. The prevailing world view in the social sciences and education is one of relativism – that there are no such things as absolute facts, and that knowledge is created and recreated by human beings. In this context, academics can tend to be rather more tolerant of each other, and each other's views, than many other groups of people.

It is fairly common for articles or books to reach different conclusions on an issue. This can be no bad thing, as it opens up issues for discussion, and encourages debate. Neither does it mean that one is absolutely correct, and the other completely wrong. Both conclusions may be right in some ways, and wrong in others. Therefore when we are comparing literature which does not come to the same conclusion, we try to be tolerant and balanced in how we express ourselves. Here are some styles of expression which might be useful in a literature review, with comments on the context in which they might be used.

> The methodological perspective of article A differs slightly from that of article B, and this may well explain the differing conclusions.

This comment avoids taking sides, but notes that the articles adopted different methodological designs, and offers this as at least a partial explanation of differences.

> The interview data in both articles is difficult to interpret. It is transcribed, as it was spoken, in dialect, and there is some uncertainty about the meanings attributed by both writers.

Here it is a question of interpretation of data. Most researchers will recognize this problem, and also accept that there are often margins for misunderstanding especially when trying to interpret dialect.

> The author of article A suggests that the evidence supports the effectiveness of a directive management style in schools, whereas the data analyzed in article B appears, according to the second author, to support a more democratic, participative approach.

The style of the comparison here is balanced and objective. It simply states in fairly neutral terms the conclusions drawn by the two authors. However, the choice of vocabulary is noteworthy. The author of article A 'suggests' rather than states, indicating an approach which is slightly tentative. Both authors use the word 'support' to refer to a particular management style, rather than stating that they definitely favour one approach or another. In addition, the second author uses the expression 'appears' to support, which again implies a rather tentative approach.

The comparison of literature is an important technique when writing a literature review. In addition, literature which reaches different conclusions concerning the same topic is not necessarily indicative of inadequacies in the way the research was conducted. Such differences in the conclusions can very often be useful points of debate in a literature review – far better sometimes than articles which appear to take a similar viewpoint.

Techniques for comparing literature which reaches different conclusions

It is not really surprising that two research studies on the same subject could reach different conclusions. A study of two separate groups of school pupils in different schools may yield completely different results. Even if the two groups were matched as far as possible for age and intelligence, there are so many potential extraneous variables, that it is very difficult to be sure that any apparent differences are valid. When you come across two pieces of literature on the same subject, which reach different conclusions, it is wise not to claim that there is indeed a major difference. It is perhaps more logical to acknowledge the difference, yet to point out the wide range of possible variables which might be having an effect upon the two studies.

Being critical of inadequacies

The same principle of relativism tends to underpin the academic writing style used to critique or criticize the content of articles or books included in a literature review. Generally speaking, when critiquing perceived inadequacies, we try to be cautious in what we say, on the grounds that we cannot be certain of the degree of inadequacy of what has been written.

In the previous sentence, the use of the phrase 'perceived inadequacies', suggests that I may not be absolutely certain whether or not there are inadequacies. Equally, the emphasis upon being 'cautious' reflects this general avoidance of sweeping statements which might give the impression of certainty. There follow some phrases which might be useful when you are being critical of inadequacies. If we think that something has been missed out of a particular article, whether that be a discussion of methodology, or perhaps some data, then we might write 'A possible omission here is . . .'. If we think that there might be a slight lack of logic in the reasoning in a research report, we might write that 'A possible logical contradiction exists in the . . .'. The use of 'possible' prevents the writer of the literature review getting into a conflict about the article, and claiming outright that it contains errors.

We can also talk about parts of the article being rather 'limited' in content. This is not too serious a criticism, and is unlikely to offend the writer of the article too much. We might suggest that the 'evidence is rather limited' in a particular argument, or that the data which is included is 'rather limited', or that the analytic process is rather limited. It is unlikely that any of these comments would make the writer of the article feel that they had written a poor article. It is probably the kind of comment which would be intended to be constructive.

On the other hand, we might say that discussion of ethical issues which are important in the research have been omitted; or that there has been an omission of any discussion of the way in which the sample was determined. This is a more direct form of criticism, and if it is factually correct, then it does call into question much more, the writing of the article. A slightly less critical phrase starts with the expression 'It tends not to explain . . .'. This might be used to say that the article or book 'tends not to explain the analytic process', or 'tends not to explain the previous research in the area'. This is a fairly mild form of criticism, which would hopefully be taken positively by the writer.

Critiquing apparent inadequacies in literature

If you wish to mount a critique of an article, it is probably best first to be as sure of your ground as possible, and, second, to write politely in measured tones. There is nothing worse than attacking an article rather vigorously, only to discover later that your arguments do not really stand up to examination! At the same time if you genuinely feel that an article is in error, then you may feel it is important for you to sound your objections. Well, you can still criticize the article, while at the same time acknowledging that you yourself may have made an error. In terms of style, you would need to write something such as: 'There is not always the space to present all of the details of sampling and data collection in a journal article, but it seems to me that there is an important omission in . . .' Or 'If I have understood the main argument in the introduction correctly, then it seems to me that there is a significant error in . . .' In this way, you can critique an article, while admitting to potential errors in your own line of reasoning.

Prose style

When discussing academic literature it is a good idea to try to be as balanced as possible in the way you reach your decisions. In other words, you should be seen as weighing up the different sides to an argument or an issue, and only then forming your viewpoint. This approach of weighing up alternatives in a fair and balanced way should be reflected in the kind of language which you use. For example, expressions such as:

The evidence would appear to indicate that . . .
On balance, it appears that . . .
As far as it is possible to discern . . .

To the extent that we can compile a full picture . . .
Weighing up the alternatives it would seem that . . .
Despite some contradictory views, it would seem that . . .
Synthesizing the main points, we might reasonably assume that . . .

all give the impression of a weighing-up of alternatives, and reaching a
balanced conclusion. When you are discussing literature it is frequently necessary to refer to writers and what they have written. It is important to have a
range of alternative expressions at your disposal, so that you do not succumb
to writing too often that 'the writer said' or 'the researcher says'. Here are
some alternatives for you to consider in your own writing.

The writer indicates that . . .
She suggests that . . .
She appears to suggest that . . .
He asserts that . . .
In the introduction he proposes that . . .
She argues that . . .
She envisages that . . .
He claims that . . .

Phrases such as these provide variety in the text, and stop the latter becoming
predictable. When the writer of an article is discussing data or evidence, we
can say:

He evaluated the evidence . . .
He analysed the evidence . . .
She compared the data . . .
She described the data . . .
He examined the data . . .
He classified the evidence . . .

Sometimes it is necessary when writing about literature to propose possible
scenarios, or to open a debate about some articles. You might then write:

It might be possible to argue . . .
It could be suggested that . . .
It is feasible that . . .
One might hypothesize that . . .
We might claim that . . .
We might consider that . . .

All of these phrases can be used to open up areas of possible discussion.
    There are some words and phrases which it is normally better to avoid in
academic prose. Some students will use the word 'discover' when writing

about the aims or purposes of research. They may write an aim such as: 'To discover the relationship between the number of hours spent in a library, and success on a degree course.' The problem with such a usage is that it implies that there is a real relationship between the two variables, and that if we approach the enquiry in the right way, we will 'unearth' this relationship somewhere. At this stage the 'relationship' is no more than an assertion or a hypothesis. It would be much more accurate to say that we are intending to explore the possible relationship between library use and degree success.

A similar type of problem exists with the word 'fact' or 'facts'. The concept of a fact implies that there exists somewhere an entity which is, in a sense, independent of human intervention. There is actually a profound philosophical issue here – that of whether entities exist independently of the human mind. Thus, we might pose the question of whether a square exists independently of the concept of a square within human consciousness. This type of problem is avoided if we simply use the term 'data' instead of facts. Thus concepts such as 'discovery' and 'facts' embrace within them philosophical assumptions which are best avoided in academic prose, unless you deliberately wish to analyze something philosophically. There are ready alternatives which do not pose unnecessary problems!

Standard approaches to referencing

When citing source materials, and using standard referencing systems, it is very easy to become immersed in the minutiae of the process, and forget the original purposes of citing books and journal articles. When writing dissertations or literature reviews, I find that students very often become almost a slave of the system of referencing, and afraid lest they should make the slightest deviation from the accepted norms. With great effort of willpower, they often manage to adhere to a system in the case of standard books and articles, but whenever they are confronted with something slightly different to cite, they can be overcome with uncertainty. As a tutor, I am often asked by a student, 'How should I reference this pamphlet or leaflet?', or perhaps some other unconventional item. The implication of the question is usually that there must be one single, correct way in which it should be done, and moreover, that I must know what that is! This is rarely the case! Perhaps it would be a good idea to review some of the basic reasons for citing sources, and the key approaches to how this can be done.

In a literature review, we need to make clear to the reader the nature of the sources we are citing. This needs to be done unambiguously, so that they are absolutely clear where sources originate, and importantly where they should go to find the original. The latter point is very important for several reasons. The reader may become interested in what we have said about a particular article or book, and wish to read it for themselves. In some cases, this is much easier today that it used to be, because of the availability of materials on the internet. The rapid speed of retrieval means that it is quite likely that readers will try to access the original. It is therefore important that we use every means at our disposal to help them in this.

Another reason for trying to help readers find the original is that all writers want to be able to justify their arguments. A key part of the underlying rationale of academic writing, and certainly of writing a literature review, is that the writer should use reasoning, arguments, and logic in such a way that the thought processes can be verified. Ultimately, the only way in which the reader can achieve this is to be able to read the original sources, and to work their way through your line of reasoning. If you are comparing two articles, for example, perhaps according to the methodology used, then if the reader is to evaluate what you are saying, it must be possible to find the original articles. In addition, readers may want to consult articles you have used, and perhaps refer to them in their own writing.

Over the years, a number of different referencing systems have evolved within the field of academic writing, and been accepted as 'standard' within certain areas or subject fields. They all include more or less the same information about the original source, with slight differences here and there. Principally, they differ in terms of layout, and where and how the information is presented in the article or literature review. Some systems make use of footnotes, while others gather the main details about the source material at the end of the literature review chapter, or at the end of the whole dissertation. There may be several reasons for selecting a particular system, but the key principle throughout your literature review is that you should be consistent. It is very confusing for your readership if you start with one system of referencing, and then deviate to another system, from time to time. It is in fact, an important principle of all writing, that you should try to think of your reader, and take into account their needs.

If you are writing your literature review as a university student, then your university will almost certainly have a policy on the referencing style to be used, and clearly it would be wise to follow this. However, it is worth noting that even within the same university, some subject departments may favour a particular style, because of the history of scholarship within that subject area. This will often be clear in the journals within that subject area. Academic journals usually contain a 'Notes for Contributors' section which provides details, among other things, of the required referencing style for that journal. If you are submitting an article to that journal, it is normally a requirement of acceptance that you have adhered to these referencing guidelines. If you are writing your literature review as part of an academic dissertation, then your supervisor will be able to advise on the most appropriate system to use.

If you have any choice at all, in terms of the referencing system to use, then there are a few broad principles which might be useful to consider. However, it should be said, that all of the main systems in use conform to these requirements to varying degrees. First of all, the system should be easy to read and to follow, for the reader. Even if the reader has not read a detailed manual on the system, it should still be possible to understand it easily. In terms of writing, it should be relatively uncomplicated to use. It should also disrupt the reading of the article as little as possible. Some people, for example, prefer a system which uses numbers in the text, while others prefer a system which cites the author's surname in the main body of the review. Finally, it is also important that the system which you employ can be adapted easily to cite unconventional items, such as leaflets or pamphlets. You may also, from time to time, need to cite literature in foreign languages, although this should not pose a problem within the main referencing systems in use.

Of the available systems, the one which appears to be most commonly used in the fields of Education and the Social Sciences, is the Harvard System. Whenever it is necessary to cite a book or article in your text, you insert the surname of the author and the year of publication. At the end of the text, all of the works cited in the text are listed in alphabetical order with full bibliographical details. Hence it is possible to locate the original. The main advantages of the Harvard System are its simplicity and lack of ambiguity. It is straightforward to use from the point of view of the academic writer, and normally does not give rise to any confusion in terms of identifying an article or book. The principal disadvantage is that the use of full surnames in the text can tend to be a little disruptive of reading if there are a lot of references. When you use a verbatim quotation from a source in your own writing, it is normal to put that quotation in italics. This helps to signify that it is taken directly from another source. In order to help the reader locate the quotation if they wish, then it is usual to put the page number on which the quotation is found in the original book or article. The citation would appear as follows in brackets at the end of the quotation (Smith, 2009, p. 36). Part of the art of academic writing is to introduce quotations and references, in such a way that your style is not repetitive. You therefore need to be inventive in your writing, while adhering sufficiently to the adopted system in order to maintain accuracy and consistency. For example, when writing your literature review, here are a few potential variations of style (fictional examples):

Professor Smith, in her widely-referenced account of medieval wall building (Smith, 2009, p. 36) suggested that . . .

or

In a detailed survey of medieval wall building, Smith (2009, p. 36) argued as follows . . .

Both of the above examples could be used where you intend to use an actual quotation. Sometimes, however, you may wish to simply note a book or article as a general source of information on the subject you are discussing. In that case, you need not cite the page number. A typical example might be:

The technical advances in wall building are suggested as a distinctive feature of the medieval period (Smith, 2009).

This would refer the reader to the book by Smith, as a general source of further information. The lack of page number indicates that the reader is simply being directed to the book for fairly general use. On the other hand, if the following were used:

Technical advances in wall building appear to have been linked with the mastery of techniques in stone trimming (Smith, 2009, p. 63).

It would suggest that there is precise information on stone trimming on page 63, even though no quotation is provided. In a literature review it may sometimes be necessary to cite a series of authors, or to group writers together. This occurs usually when you are referring to a topic on which there is a fairly extensive literature. You may decide that you do not want to select a single quotation from just one source, perhaps because it may not be sufficiently representative of what is available. You therefore can decide, if you wish, to list several examples of the kind of material which is available. You could do this in the following way:

There has been considerable research on the subject of Victorian school construction techniques (Smith, 2004; Jones, 2005; Green, 2002; Simpson, 2006).

You are trying here to give an indication of the scope of the literature which is available. You will have made value judgements about the authors and works to include. There has been no specification of page numbers and therefore it can be assumed that within these works there are general discussions of the issue of school construction in the Victorian period. The advantage of this approach in a dissertation is that it enables you to mention a large number of works in your literature review. It is a fairly widely used technique in journal articles where space is at a premium. The approach enables academics to mention a good many authors, in a short space. Sometimes, you may wish to include a short quotation of perhaps part of a sentence, in your text. In this case, there is no need to italicize the text, but merely to place it in inverted commas. The quotation would look something like this:

In a study of classroom design in Victorian schools, Jones (2001) commented on 'the bleakness of the interiors' (p. 147).

This strategy also can be useful for including more citations within a limited space. When it comes to the full list of references at the end of the literature review or dissertation, the Harvard System uses a standard format. In the case of an authored book:

James, W. (2000) *School Design and Construction Techniques*. London: Design Publishing House.

A chapter in an edited book could appear as follows:

Smith, A. (2009) The architecture of schools, in B. Johnson (ed.), *Public Buildings in the Twentieth Century*. London: Jones Publishing.

Finally, an article in an academic journal could appear as:

Smith, V. (2010) 'The expansion of universities', *Journal of Academic History*, 19(3): 124–137.

It is worth noting that within the parameters of the Harvard System, different journals, universities, and other users of the system may adopt slightly different approaches in terms of punctuation and layout of the references. The rapidly increasing practice of citing materials, which are available electronically, has introduced some complexities to the issue of referencing. These issues are considered in the next section. However, it is only possible in a book of this nature to address the broader issues of the subject of referencing. Further details are available in specialist books on the subject, as in the Key Reading section at the end of this chapter.

Citing electronic sources

Over the years a number of conventions have developed covering the citing of books and articles in academic publications. As the type of information required is fairly standard, it has not been too complex a task to agree on conventions for this. In addition, paper versions of publications are not changed very frequently, and this only tends to happen with books in the case of, for example, new editions. This enables a relative degree of consistency to be established in the case of paper-based publications.

The situation with electronic publications and sources is, however, very different. In the first place, such materials can be placed on the internet very quickly in comparison with paper-based materials. We have already mentioned the relative speed with which internet journals can publish academic articles. Besides the speed of publication, there is also the rapidity with which amendments may be made. In the case of academic journal articles, once an article has been published, it is unlikely that it will be altered, at least in the short term. However, academic material can be placed on the internet at very short notice, and also changed with increasing rapidity, as the author wishes. Another factor is the great diversity of internet source material. Within the realm of conventional citations, there are three principal types of material: authored books, chapters in edited books and academic journal articles. It is thus relatively easy to agree on styles for referencing them, and in addition publishers usually name the author of a book or chapter very clearly. However, in the case of internet materials, the sources are so diverse, that it is often very difficult to determine the author. The name of the individual who prepared the text material is very often not given, and therefore a decision has to be taken about to whom the material should be attributed. It is of course, important that a reasonable decision be taken about this, but also it is essential that whatever organization or individual is selected as the 'author', this is retained in the list of references at the end of the dissertation. The reader of the literature review will understandably expect the organization cited as the 'author' in the text to be the same at the end of the dissertation, in order that they can identify the actual source of the material, in case they wish to consult the original. Some of the difficulties of determining how to cite an electronic document may be illustrated by the following example.

On the website of BERA (British Educational Research Association) there is an electronic document entitled 'Revised Ethical Guidelines for Educational Research (2004)'. This is a document which is widely used by students and by academics, as a guide to the kind of ethical considerations which ought to be taken into account when educational research is being conducted. It is noted on the BERA website that a paper version of the document is not available, and hence it exists only in electronic form. The title page of the Ethical Guidelines document mentions the BERA organization, and one might be very tempted to use BERA as both the author and publisher. However, inside the document, on page 3, is a brief account of the history of the document and of the way in which it was developed. The latest version of the Guidelines appears to have been the outcome of a working party of three people, John Gardner, Ann Lewis and Richard Pring, with John Gardner acting as Chairperson. When they had completed their work, the document was ultimately accepted by the Council of the British Educational Research Association. There would then be an argument for treating the three working party members as the authors, with Gardner carrying pre-eminence as the chair of the working party. The form of citation in the text could thus become Gardner et al. (2004) or Gardner, Lewis and Pring (2004), and the full citation in the list of references at the end of a work could become:

Gardner, J., Lewis, A. and Pring, R. (2004) *Revised Ethical Guidelines for Educational Research (2004)* [online] available at: http://www.bera.ac.uk/ files/guidelines/ethical.pdf accessed on 18.6.11.

It is possible to recognize slight differences in style between publications, when citing electronic sources. However, essentially the same information is included. The **uniform resource locator (url)** provides the necessary information to search for the file. As it is easier to amend electronic files than paper-based files, it is normal to include the date on which the file was read. This should specify the content of the file, on that specific date.

Common pitfall

It is becoming very difficult to identify internet sites which will generally be perceived among academics as of adequate scholarly quality for a dissertation or journal article. Some internet sites, for example, are very well written by people who appear to be non-academics. Some examiners, however, have very strict views that such sites are not suitable for scholarly writing. They feel that only academic journal articles and scholarly books are appropriate. Nevertheless, academic conventions are in a state of flux, and no doubt changes will gradually develop. If, however, you use websites which are too unconventional you can probably expect criticism from examiners. Perhaps the best approach is to monitor recently-published journal articles in order to keep aware of the types of sources currently used in publications.

Calculating the number of quotations to include

A dissertation is a long and complex piece of writing. A doctoral dissertation may consist of 80,000 words or more, and a Masters dissertation may typically range from 15,000–20,000 words. It is important that the finished piece of work should be clear and coherent in structure, and that there should be a balance between the length of the different chapters. Not all the chapters will be the same length. The introductory chapter which sets the scene for the dissertation will probably be fairly brief, as will the concluding chapter which sums up the key findings. Some of the chapters in the main body of the dissertation will be considerably longer. The decisions as to the length of the individual chapters, and to their titles and content, are important. Although most dissertations have some standard structural features in common, there is room for individual creativity by the author, and the final structure will depend at least partly upon the subject matter, and the way the data was collected.

If the method of data collection was fairly straightforward and there are not too many complex issues to discuss, then the methodology chapter will be fairly brief. On the other hand this may not be the case. In some types of qualitative research, there can be many nuances to the research process, and these need to be discussed and analyzed, before the actual data is presented in the dissertation. An example is the case where a teacher or lecturer is also conducting research on education in the institution in which they teach. It is not necessarily easy to change from one role to the other, and simultaneously to take into account all the ethical issues which should be addressed, and to be faithful to the two different roles. The issues here would need addressing thoroughly in the methodology chapter.

Another important variable in social science research, which to some extent determines the structure of the dissertation, and the length of the various chapters, is whether the data collected is quantitative or qualitative. Quantitative data very often condenses into a few summary statistics, and takes up very little space. Of course, such statistics have to be analyzed and discussed, but in terms of actual space, quantitative data takes up much less space than qualitative data. In the case of the latter, there are usually numerous quotations from, say, interview transcripts. These take up a lot of space both in terms of the actual quotation extracts but also in terms of the space it takes to discuss and analyze them.

It is normal in a dissertation to devote approximately the first half of the text to a discussion of more theoretical issues such as the literature review, and the methodology. Depending upon the subject matter of the dissertation, and the preferences of the writer, these can occupy a single chapter each, or be divided into more than one chapter. Hence the literature on a subject may be, if wished, subdivided into two separate chapters. The second part of the dissertation is devoted to the presentation of the empirical data, and is divided up into a number of chapters depending upon the judgement of the writer. As a very approximate guide you can assume that after the discussion of the methodology, you are about half-way through the dissertation. However, this depends very much upon some of the issues mentioned above, such as the nature of the data, and whether or not the data collection and analysis were very complicated. If there are, for example, a great many interview quotations to be fitted into the later chapters, then this will inevitably shorten the early chapters, such as the literature review. If, on the other hand, the methodological issues to be discussed are complex, then this will lengthen the methodology chapter, and necessitate shorter chapters to present the empirical data.

Therefore, any decision concerning the number of quotations to put into the literature review depends to a large extent upon the overall structure of the rest of the dissertation, and the impact that it has on the length of the literature review chapter. Given the potential variability in dissertation structure and design, it is difficult to give any more than a very approximate estimate, but perhaps between 20–25 per cent of a dissertation could be devoted to the literature review. A dissertation is a major piece of work, often similar to an unpublished book. It therefore requires a great deal of thought and planning before writing commences. It is probably best if you plan the number of chapters in the dissertation before you begin writing, and also decide on their titles and subject matter. You will be aware of the total required length of the dissertation in words, and therefore you can then estimate the probable length of each individual chapter. For the literature review it is a fairly simple matter to calculate the length of the chapter in words. Assuming about 250 words per page, you can then estimate the number of pages in the chapter. Finally, it is a reasonable assumption that you might include an average of two quotations per page in the literature review. That will then give you the overall number of quotations needed in the chapter.

The basis of this estimate is that in a literature review, you do need to include examples of the actual writing of key authors and researchers, with the assumption that these are properly referenced. However, you do not want the chapter to consist primarily of the writing of other people! One of the main purposes of a literature review is that you demonstrate your capacity to analyze and evaluate the writing of others. You can only do this if you allow yourself sufficient space. If the quotations which you use are overly long, then they may contain too much material to discuss, and your analysis may become too superficial. If the quotations are too short, then you may not have sufficient material to discuss. The best compromise might be to select quotations which are four to five lines long, and to have about two of these per page. This should provide you with a reasonable balance between quotations and your own analytic writing.

Good practice

Remember it is important to make clear in your text which parts are quotations and which parts are your own writing. The normal way to do this is to italicize the quotations. If the quotation is three or four lines long, and you are indenting it, then it is a good idea to leave a double space at the beginning and end of the quotation. Along with the indent at the left-hand margin and the italics, this will result in the quotation standing out clearly on the page. The layout of the latter will look very professional, and the reader or examiner of your dissertation will be able to note at a glance the proportion of quotes to your text that you have used. Some people identify quotes by using a smaller font, or bold, in place of italics, although in general italics seems to be the most popular method.

Devote more space to discussing significant literature

It is one thing to calculate the number of quotations to include in the literature review chapter, but there is then the issue of how you will apportion these quotations between different research articles or books. In some cases, you might only select one quotation to use from a book, while in other cases you might use a considerable number of quotations. Much will depend upon the importance or significance which you wish to attach to an individual work. You might also decide that quotations from one author provide more material for discussion than those from a different writer. Equally, some books or articles may be well known in the field, and you may consider it necessary to spend more time and space discussing them.

All writers of literature reviews have to make decisions concerning the researchers to which they wish to give pre-eminence in the review. There are no absolutely correct answers to these decisions – it really is a matter of judgement about the researchers whom they wish to highlight in their analysis. The discussion in the previous section about the length of the review is also a key factor. Depending upon the number of words available, it may be necessary to eliminate some researchers from the discussion, simply on the basis of lack of space. We cannot expect all writers to take the same decisions about inclusion. The decision as to which researchers to include will be influenced by a number of factors such as the writer's academic background, the subjects they have studied, and the academics by whom they have been taught. Different courses and universities emphasize different approaches to a subject, and the academics will often discuss in their lectures the writers whom they feel have made the most significant contribution. Sometimes the choice of key writers to include would probably find fairly common agreement. Mauthner and Doucet (2003), for example, in a discussion of reflexivity in qualitative research, highlight the work of Norman K. Denzin. In the first section following the introduction, entitled 'The "Reflexive Turn" in the Social Sciences' (p. 416), they include three quotations from Denzin, a writer who has developed a major reputation for work in qualitative research. A number of other significant writers are also mentioned.

Key terms

Informed consent: the principle in research ethics which asserts the moral right of a potential respondent to be fully informed about a research project and their role in it, before agreeing to take part.
url (uniform resource locator): the formal term for a web address or internet address.

Key questions

1 How would you characterize an appropriate prose style for writing a literature review?

2 Why is it better to avoid the use of the word 'fact' in academic writing?
3 What are the key problems when citing electronic sources?

Key reading

Gillett, A., Hammond, A. and Martala, M. (2009) *Successful Academic Writing.* Harlow: Pearson Education.

Neville, C. (2010) *The Complete Guide to Referencing and Avoiding Plagiarism,* 2nd edn. Maidenhead: Open University Press.

Pears, R. and Shields, G. (2010) *Cite Them Right: The Essential Referencing Guide*, 8th edn. Basingstoke: Palgrave Macmillan.

Swales, J. and Feak, C.B. (2004) *Academic Writing for Graduate Students: Essential Tasks and Skills*, 2nd edn. Ann Arbor, MI: The University of Michigan Press.

Wallace, M. and Wray, A. (2006) *Critical Reading and Writing for Postgraduates*. London: Sage.

8

Relating the review to the rest of the dissertation

Summary

It is important that a literature review is not perceived as a self-standing chapter in a dissertation – an end in itself. It is an important element in the overall report of the research. It should set the research in context, explaining some of the key work which has been conducted previously, and showing how the current research builds upon that. The literature review is also very useful for identifying areas which could form the basis of future research. Primarily though, it acts as a means of linking together the different parts of the dissertation. It is always possible for you, whichever part of the dissertation you are writing, to look back at the literature which has been discussed, and to draw upon it for further analysis. This chapter examines the different ways in which the literature review can act as a link throughout the dissertation. Moreover, it is worth considering that the dissertation you are presently writing, will one day itself become part of someone else's literature review!

Learning outcomes

After reading this chapter you should be able to do the following:

- Demonstrate how your study is connected with previous studies.
- Relate the literature review to research questions and aims.
- Link findings and results with the literature review.

Questions for further research

A good literature review not only provides a sound bedrock for the current dissertation, but can also provide an inspiration for future students who are considering starting a research degree. On the one hand, a literature review may identify significant gaps in research, which might suggest future investigations. In addition, however, a good literature review may be so interesting to future students that they will want to conduct a similar study in perhaps a slightly different context. A good literature review gathers together into one place, all the significant work on a topic, and that in itself is a valuable function. It enables someone else to gain a quick, all-round impression of a subject, when to do this for themselves would take a long time.

Research can be conducted for a variety of reasons, and there are many factors which motivate students to select a particular topic and to pursue an investigation of it. Some of these factors include:

- the desire to solve a particular issue or problem;
- the wish to acquire knowledge and extend their understanding of a topic;
- the need to acquire new skills such as questionnaire design or designing a survey;
- an intrinsic interest in a subject;
- the wish to acquire qualifications and pursue an academic or other career;
- a desire to be involved in research activities.

A literature review can assist in all of these objectives. First of all, it provides the reader with an overview of the kind of issues and problems which exist in a subject area. When trying to define a research topic and develop a research design, many students find it easy to think of a broad topic which interests them, but find it very difficult to identify a suitable research topic. A student might be interested in environmental issues, for example, but cannot distil this subject down to a specific research question which could form the basis for a study. A literature review, however, because it gives details of many research studies in an area, can provide ideas for possible research topics. It can also give an idea of the general scope of the research being currently done in a subject. This can also help students gain an idea of how they can go about extending their knowledge in a subject. A psychology student may have been exposed in their education to experimental studies, and to the study of motivation and cognitive development. A literature review may, however, lead them on to new areas of the subject, such as humanistic psychology. By reading articles referred to in this new area, they may again develop ideas for future research.

A literature review can also be very useful in providing you with ideas for structuring a new research project. It is one thing to define a research question, but quite another to plan the collection and analysis of data. You need to decide how to identify a group of respondents, and then to determine if it is necessary to take a sample of these. All of these questions contain both theoretical and practical questions which need to be resolved. It is also very difficult for inexperienced researchers to anticipate all of the potential problems in this planning process. A literature review can help enormously, because it brings together examples of different research, all of which will have a slightly different approach to methodology. You may be able to select a particular article which will help you devise your own approach to research methods. The literature review can also be very helpful in enabling new researchers to familiarize themselves with the use of data collection methods such as questionnaires. Articles reviewed may contain examples of research questionnaires or interview schedules which can inform the design of new data collection instruments.

Literature reviews are very useful reading for young researchers who are beginning to define their own field of research.

Projecting forward to new research areas

Academics generally build their careers around a particular research interest. This process usually starts with the subject matter of their doctoral dissertation, and continues in a number of ways. They attend conferences related to that subject; make bids for research funds to continue their research interests; give talks in the media; and publish journal articles and books. All of this is predicated, however, on being up-to-date with the research currently being conducted in the subject area, via such means as literature reviews. This enables the aspiring academic to plan future areas of research, and to develop a rational career pathway.

By reading a review, the young academic can get a sense of the kind of topics which are currently being researched, and through a reading of some of the articles and books, can begin to construct a career pathway for themselves. Academic researchers do tend to concentrate on a particular research topic, since in this way they can develop a specialism, and become known as an expert in a specific field. Trying to develop such a specialism is not necessarily easy, and the reading of literature reviews can help in this regard.

Connecting the literature review with other parts of the dissertation

Sometimes students think of the literature review as a little bit of a formality – something which is a requirement, and therefore they carry it out, but would rather prefer to get on with presenting and analyzing their research data!

However, the literature review is at the heart of a dissertation, and care should be taken to make sure it interconnects with all the other sections of the dissertation. The basic reason for this is that the literature review provides the basis for the current research. It establishes the nature of the ground on which the current dissertation is built – rather like the foundations of a building. The new research should sit firmly on the foundations of the literature review, with the result that the reader of the dissertation will be able to understand the continuity in the creation of knowledge and ideas.

Demonstrating how your study is connected with previous studies

When some students are developing a research project, they feel that it is necessary to think very independently, and to develop a topic which no one else has even remotely investigated! Perhaps some are overly concerned with developing a unique contribution to knowledge, and hence want to steer clear of any previous research. Generally speaking, however, this ambition is a little unrealistic. The amount of research being carried out in the social sciences is so extensive, and is growing exponentially, that it is difficult to identify a topic which is entirely new, and has never been explored before. From time to time there are new research studies which open up fresh perspectives in a discipline, but it is rare that a research student is able to do this. It is much more usual that a student will study carefully the previous research which has been carried out, and then develop a research proposal which builds upon that.

There are, however, possible exceptions to this. Young people, much more than older, established researchers, have been brought up and educated in a rapidly moving world of computers, the internet, and electronic communication. The rapidly developing nature of this world, and the fact that established researchers may be less familiar with it than research students, mean that it is an area where it can be relatively easy to design new and interesting research projects.

An example of such research is the study by Pasche (2008) of the use of video sharing websites in the study of religions. In particular she concentrates upon methodological issues in using such material. The vast quantity and variety of material on the internet has scarcely been utilized as research data so far, and there are extensive opportunities to examine it in a variety of research projects. It may help to briefly mention one or two issues raised by Pasche in order to give the flavour of the kind of project which it would be possible to devise.

The first issue (p. 2) is not just one which concerns video sharing sites, but also other sites which have religious or indeed material on any other subject. This issue is whether the researcher reveals their true identity and purpose. The researcher has the alternative on the one hand of revealing their occupation as researcher, of revealing their identity when contributing to discussion groups, and of being completely open about any purposes they have in relation to entering the website concerned. On the other hand, the researcher could hide their own identity, not participate at all in the activities or conversations on the site, and in general try to maintain what we might term the 'social ecological validity' of the internet site. As the internet is changing so rapidly, and as we all have our own favoured approaches to using the internet for research, it is very difficult to evaluate these strategies in absolute terms. Certainly, however, there is a very wide range of possibilities for research here. A second issue in the use of such sites for research is the question of language (p. 3). As Pasche points out, some but not all of the videos use English as the principal language, and this can create some difficulties in terms of understanding and interpreting. Anyway, there would appear to be enormous potential in this type of study for young researchers. The latter are normally very familiar with the internet, and it only needs a little imagination to create a novel idea for a research study. There are some existing studies, and hence this kind of topic has in a sense, the best of both worlds. A research topic can be stimulated by an existing dissertation or article; yet at the same time, there is so much potential data available, that the research student can relatively easily define a new idea for a study.

Relate literature to research questions and aims

A dissertation has to have a sense of direction. In order to plan the research design effectively, you need to have a clear understanding of what you hope to analyze, investigate, explore or examine. All of your key decisions will stem from the research questions and aims which you have established.

Good practice

When you have written your aims or objectives for your research, have them read and checked by at least two experienced researchers. The aims need to be precisely worded, achievable, and, very importantly, have a sound academic, intellectual content. In other words, they should aim to add something to our knowledge and understanding of the world. In this case, they will be able to lead on to a significant area of literature which can be reviewed.

Based upon the things you hope to achieve in your research, you will probably take a number of important decisions such as the following.

- how to structure your literature review;
- the overall theoretical perspective which will underpin the research study;
- the type of data collection method which will be used;
- the ethical concerns which it will be important to address in the study;
- the method of analyzing the data;
- the way in which a theory will be constructed or tested;
- the extent to which the original research aims have been met;
- the original contribution to knowledge.

One of the earliest of these decisions is the relationship between the aims of the dissertation and the nature of the literature review. Now it is worth reflecting that decisions about the literature review do not follow entirely sequentially from the aims of the dissertation. In other words, the nature of the literature review does not, and should not really, depend upon the aims. In reality, there should be a kind of equilibrium between the two. The research student should ideally proceed roughly as follows.

The first step is to define the research topic and then try to identify as precisely as possible, several aims for the research. Let us suppose that the general area for the investigation is the standard of English among higher education students. Further, let us assume that the aims of the study are initially defined as follows:

- to examine whether the standard of English among undergraduate students is changing;

- to analyze various potential causes for any change;
- to propose strategies for improving the standard of English among undergraduates.

The next step would be to conduct an initial, and probably fairly broad survey of the kind of academic literature available for the literature review. It may be as a result of this that you are unhappy with the quantity of material available. Perhaps you find suitable material on study skills in higher education and also on strategies designed to help students with their language skills and academic writing, but less on research into changing standards of English. As a result of this you begin to wonder whether there is sufficient material available for the aims of the thesis in their present form. You decide to re-structure the aims in order to concentrate on the teaching and support strategies to help students with their writing skills. The purpose of the study is to do the following:

- to review the methods and procedures adopted to help undergraduates with their academic English writing;
- to analyze the types of errors typically made by undergraduates in their academic writing;
- to examine the perceptions of students concerning the type of help they need in order to improve their writing.

The process would then be repeated with the new aims. You would conduct an initial review of materials available, and then decide whether it was realistic to continue with the existing aims. In other words it is wise from the beginning of a dissertation or research study to see the different elements of it as inter-related. As the aims will have such far-reaching consequences for the study, it is best to go through a phase of evaluation and revision, before deciding upon the final wording.

It is worth noting, however, that it is not only the literature review and the aims which are inter-connected, but the aims and the data collection process. For example, the first of the revised aims will probably require access to several different colleges and universities for the collection of data. It may require access to study skills tutors and also to students, in order to establish the nature of current provision for help with academic writing. Before finalizing the aims, therefore, it is important to consider also the relationship with methodology. If it is not possible to collect the necessary data to fulfil a set of aims, then the latter will require revising, and those revised aims will in turn affect the literature as mentioned before. The more we explore this issue, we realize that there is a close relationship between all these elements of the dissertation, and that a change in one of the factors has an immediate consequence for others.

It is important, therefore, to take a holistic view of a research study. It would in a way be reassuring to think of research as a series of isolated stages or steps.

It might be easier for our brains to handle research in this way, but it does not really represent accurately the reality of the situation. To employ that much-used metaphor, research and dissertation writing require us to keep lots of balls in the air at the same time. We have to be continually flexible in our thinking, and be prepared to adapt our strategy as circumstances change.

Linking findings and results with the literature review

It is generally seen as a good idea to be able to make some kind of link between your research results and the articles you have discussed in your literature review. Contrary to what many research students believe, it is not necessary to try to make a dramatic discovery, to gain a Masters degree or doctorate. In fact, it is very difficult to make an advance in knowledge of such proportions. A researcher should normally feel happy by making a small addition to our knowledge on a particular issue. Indeed, research largely consists of incremental additions to our existing knowledge. It is here that the essential relationship lies, between findings and results, and the literature which has been discussed in the review. It is often expected that the research findings will to some extent at least build upon research which has been completed before.

One of the advantages to this is that it helps to create a cohesion within the dissertation, so that there is a clear relationship between previous findings and the new research. In terms of writing the dissertation, this is done in chronological order, and therefore it is not possible to discuss the findings within the literature review chapter. The data may have all been collected and analyzed by the time you are writing the literature review, but it will scarcely be possible to mention any of this. There is usually a clear demarcation between the first half of the dissertation and the second half. The literature review and the methodology are discussed in the first half, and in this there is very rarely any primary data. The latter is then presented in the second half of the dissertation.

In effect, then, the links between the findings and results have to be made in retrospect. Where some data, or analysis, appears to relate to examples within the literature review, mention can be made of this in the appropriate data analysis chapter. When this is being done, it is a good idea to think about the reader of your dissertation. This reader may be your examiner or they may be future research students who have accessed your dissertation for help when they are preparing their own research proposal. It will be a great help to your reader, if when cross-referencing something from the data chapters, you mention the precise paragraph, sub-section or page number within the literature review. It is also worth bearing in mind that as you move towards the final version of your dissertation that the page numbers will probably change. Therefore, with regard to cross-referencing sections to the literature review, it may be worth waiting until very near the end of the writing before inserting the page references.

Common pitfall

On this particular point, there are many advantages in maintaining each chapter of a dissertation, including the literature review, as a separate file, with or without page numbering. The main advantage of this is that when you make some amendments to one chapter, it does not alter the page numbering in any other chapter. Normally, when the dissertation is saved as one single, large file, even quite small changes of one or two sentences can cause a chapter heading, say, to move half-way down a page. This means that any cross-referencing can easily be rendered inaccurate. Where separate files are used, this does not happen. All that is necessary is that files should be page-numbered sequentially once the dissertation is completed.

Relating primary data of research to the literature review

Primary data is, by its very nature, often specific to the research context. It is therefore not necessarily very easy to compare it from one situation to another. The conclusions and analysis of research can be compared, but only limited comparisons can be made with the data itself. Having said that, there are some differences between qualitative and quantitative data in terms of comparison. If we are comparing our own research data with an article from the literature review, then quantitative data may simply be a matter of comparing tables of raw data, and this may not be very fruitful. However, there are potentially a few differences which might emerge from the comparison of qualitative data. Suppose that our own study concerns interviews with school teachers, as does an article in the literature review. The data could differ in a variety of ways, even though the respondents are all teachers, yet come from two different samples.

- Some teachers may be very talkative, generating a lot of data, while others may say relatively little.
- Some may be enthusiastic about the state of the teaching profession, while others are negative and pessimistic.

- Some may be articulate and analytic in what they say, while others put things rather briefly and do not make many comments.
- Some may express a wish to stay in the classroom as teachers, while others indicate that they would like to gain management posts.
- Some see themselves as staying in education for all of their careers, while others anticipate they would like a career change within a few years.

With this type of data there could therefore be some points of comparison or difference between the two pieces of research. However, the contexts of the two pieces of research could be very different.

- The schools in the two pieces of research could be very different.
- The catchment areas could differ.
- The social background of the pupils may be very different.
- One may be an urban school and the other rural.
- The schools may differ in size.

Hence any comparisons may be of superficial significance. Nevertheless, it would be useful to relate raw data gathered to similar data from the literature review.

Another technique of comparison would be to contrast the way in which the data is presented, in terms of transcription style. Interview data or focus group data is usually transcribed prior to being used in a dissertation or research article. It is easier for the researcher to make sense of the data, and extracts can more easily be selected to include as quotations, and to be analysed within the research. However, there are a number of different ways in which the interview recordings can be transcribed. If the researcher is interested in the broad sense of what has been said, then it is simply a matter of transcribing the words that were used, with a relatively small amount of punctuation. All that is required is a sufficient number of commas and full stops to ensure that the essence of the original meaning is conveyed. However, in some kinds of research, notably ethnomethodological research, there is a tendency to transcribe in a very detailed way, using varieties of diacritical marks to indicate the way in which words were spoken. For example, words which were emphasized by the speaker would be identified in a certain way, and pauses in the spoken word would also be indicated. Indeed, pauses of different length would be marked as such. The idea behind this detail of transcription is to try to enable the researcher to draw conclusions about, for example, the emotion behind certain utterances. A comparison between your data and the way in which transcription had taken place in the literature review articles would enable judgements to be made about the types of conclusions which could be drawn from the different types of data.

Another interesting aspect of data which could be a useful point of comparison with your literature review is the way in which the context of the data is explained. All data is collected in a specific social context, which may have a greater or lesser effect upon the nature of the data. Suppose you are interviewing a group of employees about what it is like to work in their organization. You might interview some in an informal setting of a bar or café, well away from the workplace, while others are interviewed in the workplace, within earshot of their line manager's office. Most people would probably expect the data to be slightly different! However, even without the intervention of line managers into the setting, simply the everyday situation in which the data was collected can provide an interesting background to the research. If you are collecting data in a school, it is interesting to document and describe the type of school building, its immediate environment, the facilities it possesses, the first impression when you walk into the school, the type of sports facilities available, and anything else which you feel helps to build up a picture of the school. Much the same applies to any employment organization, or to a social setting where data is being collected. A description such as this helps to 'bring the data alive', and to help readers of your dissertation appreciate the context in which the data was collected. It helps to give 'meaning' to the data. Not all researchers provide this type of contextual information, although it is generally the norm within ethnographic research. A comparison of the way in which you establish the research setting for your data with the methods used within the literature review articles can form an interesting study, and be worth commenting on.

When qualitative data is used in a research study, it is very rare that the whole of the data is used. The researcher normally makes a selection from the considerable amount of interview transcripts or other data. If we imagine a recording of an interview, for example, there will be a considerable amount of the record which consists of pleasantries between researcher and respondent, or verbal exchanges which merely serve to help the conversation move along. As research data for analysis, the researcher is only interested in the parts which involve discussion of substantive issues. Even among these sections of discussion, some parts of the interviews may appear more significant than others and hence better suited to analysis.

Now this selection of data may not be made uniformly across all the respondents who took part in the study. Suppose for the sake of argument that there are 30 respondents in a study. By the time the researcher has selected the extracts from the interviews which are seen as being most interesting or relevant to the study, only a relatively small proportion of those 30 respondents may be significantly represented. Perhaps the majority of the data selected for inclusion may come from, say, ten respondents, with only small amounts from another third, and none at all from the remainder. This may not happen in all cases of research, but it could easily happen in some.

Now when data is being written up as an article or dissertation, it is quite common for the writer to first of all describe the sample of interviewees, and also the number of interviewees. The quotations from the transcripts are then presented and analysed, without any mention of which individual respondent provided each quotation. In other words, the sample of respondents are treated as if they were an amorphous whole, who generated the data used. This does not in a sense seem entirely satisfactory. It would appear much more rational to distinguish the respondents in some way, and then to indicate from which respondent each element of data came. For example, if each of the respondents were given a number from 1–30, and then after each quotation in the article or dissertation a number was used to indicate the respondent, it would be possible for the reader to gain an accurate impression of the distribution of data between respondents. This would enable the reader to see if the data selection was significantly skewed within the sample. It would be interesting to compare your research study in this respect with studies in the literature review. If you wished to be even more precise, you could identify a number of characteristics of your respondents, such as gender, age range, and the numbering system above, and include these details after each quotation. For example, (M, 20–30, 17) would provide basic information which the reader could relate to the content of the data quotation. There is a variety of ways in which this could be done, including the use of pseudonyms. Such a system would help the reader to judge the extent to which all members of the research sample were included in the research report.

In some dissertations a sample of raw data is included in the appendix, and this sometimes enables the reader to appreciate the nature of the data better than simply reading short extracts. One can gain an impression of the flow of the conversation during an interview, and also perhaps appreciate better the decisions which had to be made by the researcher in terms of selecting data for analysis. It is, however, usually much easier to do this in a dissertation than a journal article, simply because of the greater availability of space. In some articles, however, the writer may manage to include one or two pages of raw data in the appendix, in order to give the flavour of the research. It is then possible to compare the dissertation data with that in articles within the literature review. Where an interview schedule was employed in the research, it is also usually the norm to include a copy of this in the appendix of a dissertation. This provides a detailed picture of the type of questions which were asked and the sequence of questions. It enables the reader to grasp much more precisely the nature of the interview process. However, interview schedules are not always included in the appendices of journal articles, usually for reasons of space, although where they are included, they can form a useful basis for comparison.

It is normal for reasons of research ethics, to try as far as possible to preserve the anonymity of respondents in research studies. This is normally done by using pseudonyms, or code numbers, to indicate respondents. Sometimes, however, it is difficult to be absolutely certain that the anonymity of a respondent has been preserved because certain aspects of their life may be included which reveal their possible identity. A fairly common example of this is where the job role or employment of a person is discussed. This can sometimes give a relatively strong indication of their identity. On the other hand, however, it is often very relevant to the research study to provide a few biographical details of respondents. These can help a great deal in enabling the reader of a research study to understand the data and the research conclusions. It is often necessary though to reach an effective compromise between the advantages of providing some biographical data, and the need to take reasonable care to preserve anonymity. The nature of biographical data does provide a useful focus of comparison between qualitative research studies.

Finally, the comparison of quantitative data does provide slightly different issues to that of qualitative data. Some of the points of comparison may include:

- the mechanism for selecting the sample;
- the choice of statistical tests to be used;
- the presentation of the results of such tests;
- the presentation of descriptive statistics in the form of tables, graphs, or spreadsheets;
- the way in which conclusions are drawn.

Comparisons between the main research study and those mentioned in a literature review may revolve around technical matters such as the selection of an appropriate statistical test. In addition, sample sizes may be different, and this may reduce the relevance of a comparison. However, it is important with any type of research, and particularly in terms of the mathematical and statistical nature of quantitative research, that the reasoning process of the data analysis is made as transparent as possible. The degree to which this is done can form a useful basis of comparison.

Types of methodology used in previous research

In a purist sense the methodology of a research study should be determined by the aims of the study. The aims establish the parameters of the study, and the method which will be used then follows from those aims. The method is selected depending upon the nature of the research problem. Broadly speaking, if the purpose of the research study is to develop an understanding of general trends in society, then quantitative survey methods will probably be required; on the other hand, if a more in-depth study is anticipated, then qualitative methods may seem more appropriate.

The aims are not, however, usually written in a vacuum. The researcher does not write the aims with no knowledge at all of where they might logically lead. When writing the aims, the researcher is usually thinking in parallel about the consequences of that decision. There are cases, however, where a researcher makes a decision in advance concerning the type of methodology to use, and then writes the aims as something of an afterthought. There is nothing really wrong with this, providing the aims and the methodology match. There are some researchers, however, who for various reasons develop a favourite methodology, say, ethnography or action research, and then stick to this irrespective of the research questions they are addressing. This is clearly a mistake, and does not lead to a coherent piece of research. Again, there is nothing wrong with developing a personal interest and expertise in a particular type of research, as long as it is used to address relevant problems. This then provides one point of comparison between a research study and the works which are discussed in a literature review. You can examine the aims of a range of studies from the literature review, and analyze the extent to which the selected methodology is appropriate. If it does not seem entirely appropriate, then this begs a variety of questions, including the reason for the choice of methodology.

Another way in which research studies can be compared in terms of methodology, is the extent to which the methodology is employed in an accurate and valid way. For example, a variety of different studies may be described as participant observation research, and yet this may only be accurate to a range of different extents. If a teacher is collecting data in a class of students while teaching, then this may be a genuine participant observation study. On the other hand, a researcher who simply visits a school to collect data may not be 'participating' to any realistic extent. For many research studies, there is a question to be asked about the extent to which the 'label' attached to the study is accurate or justifiable. This provides a useful point of comparison when discussing the range of studies included in the literature review.

Other examples where methodological terms may not be employed quite as precisely as they might be include ethnography, **case study research** and **life history research**. One of the key purposes of ethnographic research is to gain an insight into the world as seen by the respondent. The world is not seen as a series of social facts as defined by the researcher, but as the creation of those people involved in the world. If we want to understand the world of a police officer, for example, we do not write about it as we imagine their life to be. On the contrary, we ask police officers about their perceptions of their lives, and we try to put ourselves in their position. We observe them during their daily lives, and ask them about the pressures and difficulties which they experience. In this way we construct an 'ethnography' of their lives, which tries to represent their existence as faithfully as possible. Ethnographies can be compared to the degree that they genuinely try to view the world through the eyes of the social actors who make up the context being studied. This forms a basis for contrasting research studies in the literature review with the dissertation study.

A research case study can consist of almost anything from an institution such as a school or college, to an individual person, or to a group of people who are linked together through a work or social context. However, a case study should not be simply selected at random. There should be something about a case study which makes it worthy of being singled out for a research study. In some situations, it may be that the case study is very 'ordinary'. In other words it seems to manifest characteristics which appear relatively typical of its type. Such a case study might be useful in terms of revealing something of the everyday life of a social situation. On the other hand, the case study might be 'extreme' in some way. It might be atypical, and hence by its unusual nature, reveal distinct features of the topic under study. For example, a case study of a school in an extremely deprived social area may reveal something of the difficulties children experience in learning in such a situation, and indeed of teachers being able to teach in a context such as that. To take a contrary example, a case study of a private boarding school would be likely to reveal a very different perspective on the education system. A comparison of the way case studies are selected in a dissertation and in the literature review often provides a useful point of contrast.

Finally, life history research can be compared in terms of the criteria used to select people for study. It is certainly not necessary to select someone celebrated or well known to be the subject of life history research. Indeed, it is sometimes more appropriate to select someone who has led an 'ordinary' life. One of the key purposes of life history research is to relate the life of an individual person to the main social trends which have taken place during their lifetime. A life history should not therefore be simply a chronological sequence of the main events of a life, but a much more complex account of the way individual lives inter-relate with the great social, political and economic forces which mould our existence. The extent to which life history research is able to do this is a measure of its quality. This provides a useful means of comparing a literature review of life history research with a dissertation.

Recent developments in the subject area

One of the essential functions of a literature review is that it should construct an account of the most recent research in a subject area. It should weave together the latest research into a coherent account in order to provide a sense of the direction in which a subject area is developing. This then allows the researcher who is writing a dissertation to describe his or her own research in terms of the extent to which it is built upon existing knowledge.

This is very important, as arguably the key criterion used to judge the quality of doctoral research is whether it makes an original contribution to knowledge. When you have submitted your doctoral dissertation you will be assessed partly on the dissertation, but you will also have to respond to questions in an oral examination or viva voce. The purpose of this is partly so that you can provide evidence of your knowledge of research methodology in an unrehearsed and spontaneous situation, and demonstrate that the work of the dissertation is your own work. However, in one form or another, you will also be asked to explain the extent to which your research has contributed something original to the field in which you have been working. This is where the literature review is essential. Your starting point in order to make out your case of an original contribution will need to be an explanation of the progress in your chosen field, up to the point of the commencement of your research. You will then need to explain clearly the way in which your research has added to this pre-existing knowledge. The examiners will not be expecting to hear about a new theory of universal relativity! They will simply wish to hear you explain how your research has added something incremental to your chosen field of knowledge. In order to do this, you will need to return to your literature review, and then show how your research has added to this.

This perhaps demonstrates more than anything else, the central importance of a writing a good literature review. Happy reviewing!

Key terms

Case study research: a form of qualitative or mixed method research, which selects a single example of a phenomenon to investigate and from which to generalize to some extent.

Ethnomethodology: a form of qualitative research which examines in detail the language which we use, and how this can be analysed in order to understand something of the way in which we construct meaning out of the social world.

Life history research: a form of qualitative research which takes as its subject the life of an individual, and relates this to the wider context of society.

Key questions

1 In what ways should the literature review develop from the aims of a research study?
2 What strategies can you use to make a connection between the methodology of your dissertation and the methodology of the works discussed in the literature review?
3 In what way are recent developments outlined in the literature review, connected with the need to make an original contribution to knowledge?

Key reading

Bassey, M. (1999) *Case Study Research in Educational Settings*. Maidenhead: Open University Press.

Burton, D. and Bartlett, S. (2009) *Key Issues for Education Researchers*. London: Sage.

Goodson, I.F. and Sikes, P. (2001) *Life History Research in Educational Settings: Learning from Lives*. Maidenhead: Open University Press.

Lichtman, M. (2010) *Understanding and Evaluating Qualitative Educational Research*. London: Sage.

Pole, C. and Morrison, M. (2003) *Ethnography for Education*. Maidenhead: Open University Press.

References

ALARA (2010) *Action Learning and Action Research Association*, [online] available at: http://www.alara.net.au/public/home, accessed on 12.5.11.

American Psychological Association (2011) *PsycINFO®*, [online] available at: http://www.apa.org/pubs/databases/psycinfo/index.aspx, accessed on 4.5.11, accessed on 12.5.11.

American Sociological Review (2011) *American Sociological Review*, [online] available at: http://www.asanet.org/journals/asr/index.cfm, accessed on 13.5.11.

Apple, M.W. (2008) Can schooling contribute to a more just society? *Education, Citizenship and Social Justice*, 3(3): 239–61.

ASA (2011) *American Sociological Association, ASA*, [online] available at: http://www.asanet.org/, accessed on 13.5.11.

Australian Psychological Society (2011) *Australian Psychological Society*, [online] available at: http://www.psychology.org.au/, accessed on 15.5.11.

BERA (2011) *British Educational Research Association*, [online] available at: http://www.bera.ac.uk/, accessed on 15.5.11.

Bloglines® (2011) *Bloglines®*, [online] available at: http://www.bloglines®.com/, accessed on 19.4.11.

British Library (2011a) *British Library*, [online] available at: http://www.bl.uk/, accessed on 29.4.11.

British Library (2011b) *EthOS-Beta: Electronic Theses Online Service*, [online] available at: http://ethos.bl.uk/, accessed on 3.5.11.

Brown, J. and Sadler, K. (2010) *Impact on Future Publication*. London: University College, London.

Bullough, R.V. Jr. and Pinnegar, S. (2001) Guidelines for quality in autobiographical forms of self-study research, *Educational Researcher*, 30(3): 13–21.

Buzan, T. (2010) *The Mind Map® Book: Unlock Your Creativity, Boost Your Memory, Change Your Life*. Harlow: BBC Active.

Carter, S.M. and Little, M. (2007) Justifying knowledge, justifying method, taking action: epistemologies, methodologies, and methods in qualitative research, *Qualitative Health Research*, 17(10): 1316–28.

Cho, J. and Trent, A. (2006) Validity in qualitative research revisited, *Qualitative Research*, 6(3): 319–40.

Copac® (2010) *Copac®*, [online] available at: http://copac.ac.uk, accessed on 29.4.11.

Cornell University (2011) *arXiv*, [online] available at: http://arxiv.org/, accessed on 11.4.11.

Costa, M.V. (2006) Galston on liberal virtues and the aims of civic education, *Theory and Research in Education*, 4(3): 275–89.

Czymoniewicz-Klippel, M.T., Brijnath, B. and Crockett, B. (2010) Ethics and the promotion of inclusiveness within qualitative research: case examples from Asia and the Pacific, *Qualitative Inquiry*, 16(5): 332–41.

Dickson-Swift, V., James, E.L., Kippen, S. and Liamputtong, P. (2007) Doing sensitive research: what challenges do qualitative researchers face? *Qualitative Research*, 7(3): 327–53.

EBSCO (2011) *Education Abstracts*, [online] available at: http://www.ebscohost.com/corporate/education-abstracts, accessed on 4.5.11.

Elsevier B.V. (2011) *SciVerse® Scopus*, [online] available at: http://www.info.sciverse.com/scopus, accessed on 3.5.11.

Emerald Group (2011) *Leadership and Organization Development Journal*, [online] available at: http://www.emeraldinsight.com/products/journals/journals.htm?id=lodj, accessed on 9.4.11.

Erel, U. (2010) Migrating cultural capital: Bourdieu in migration studies, *Sociology* 44(4): 642–60.

European Commission (2011) *Research and Innovation*, [online] available at: http://ec.europa.eu/research/index.cfm, accessed on 19.4.11.

European Educational Research Association (2011) *European Educational Research Association*, EERA, [online] available at: http://www.eera-ecer.eu/news/, accessed on 15.5.11.

Freshwater, D., Cahill, J., Walsh, E. and Muncey, T. (2010) Qualitative research as evidence: criteria for rigour and relevance, *Journal of Research in Nursing*, 15(6): 497–508.

Freytes Frey, A. and Cross, C. (2011) Overcoming poor youth stigmatization and invisibility through art: a participatory action research experience in Greater Buenos Aires, *Action Research*, 9(1): 65–82.

Gardner, J., Lewis, A. and Pring, R. (2004) *Revised Ethical Guidelines for Educational Research (2004)*, [online] available at: http://www.bera.ac.uk/files/guidelines/ethical.pdf, accessed on 18.6.11.

Google™Scholar (2011) *Google™Scholar*, [online] available at: http://scholar.google.co.uk/, accessed on 29.4.11.

GreyNet International (2011) *GreyNet: Grey Literature Network Service*, [online] available at: http://www.greynet.org/, accessed on 12.4.11.

Hedenus, A. (2011) Finding prosperity as a Lottery winner: presentations of self after acquisition of sudden wealth, *Sociology*, 45(1): 22–37.

Institute of Education Sciences (2011) *ERIC*, [online] available at: http://www.eric.ed.gov/, accessed on 10.5.11.

Iversen, R.R. (2009) 'Getting out' in ethnography: a seldom-told story, *Qualitative Social Work*, 8(1): 9–26.

Jackson, C. and Tinkler, P. (2001) Back to basics: a consideration of the purposes of the PhD viva, *Assessment and Evaluation in Higher Education*, 26(4): 355–66.

Kelly, S., White, M.I., Martin, D. and Rouncefield, M. (2006) Leadership refrains: patterns of leadership, *Leadership*, 2(2): 181–201.

Kiley, M. and Mullins, G. (2005) Examining the examiners: how inexperienced examiners approach the assessment of research theses, *International Journal of Educational Research*, 41: 121–35.

Kinsler, K. (2010) The utility of educational action research for emancipatory change, *Action Research*, 8(2): 171–89.

Lever, J. (2011) Urban regeneration partnerships: a figurational critique of governmentality theory, *Sociology*, 45(1): 86–101.

Maginn, P.J. (2007) Towards more effective community participation in urban regeneration: the potential of collaborative planning and applied ethnography, *Qualitative Research*, 7(1): 25–43.

Mauthner, N.S. and Doucet, A. (2003) Reflexive accounts and accounts of reflexivity in qualitative data analysis, *Sociology*, 37(3): 413–31.

McGibbon, E., Peter, E. and Gallop, R. (2010) An institutional ethnography of nurses' stress, *Qualitative Health Research*, 20(10): 1353–78.

Murthy, D. (2008) Digital ethnography: an examination of the use of new technologies for social research, *Sociology*, 42(5): 837–55.

NFER (2011) *The National Foundation for Educational Research in England and Wales*, [online] available at: http://www.nfer.ac.uk/index.cfm, accessed on 15.5.11.

OpenSIGLE (2011) *System for Information on Grey Literature in Europe*, [online] available at: http://opensigle.inist.fr/, accessed on 12.4.11.

Pasche, F. (2008) Some methodological reflections about the study of religions on video sharing websites, *Marburg Journal of Religion*, 13(1): 1–10.

SCONUL (2009) *Society of College, National and University Libraries*, [online] available at: http://www.sconul.ac.uk/, accessed on 29.4.11.

Shah, B., Dwyer, C. and Modood, T. (2010) Explaining educational achievement and career aspirations among young British Pakistanis: mobilizing 'ethnic capital'?, *Sociology*, 44(6): 1109–27.

Social Science Electronic Publishing (2011) *Social Science Research Network (SSRN)*, [online] available at: http://www.ssrn.com/home_bd.html, accessed on 9.5.11.

SPARC (2011) *Scholarly Publication and Academic Resources Coalition (SPARC)*, [online] available at: http://www.arl.org/sparc/index.shtml, accessed on 12.4.11.

Thomson Reuters (2011a) *Conference Proceedings Citation Index*, [online] available at: http://thomsonreuters.com/products_services/science/science_products/a-z/conf_proceedings_citation_index/, accessed 12.4.11.

Thomson Reuters (2011b) *EndNote*, [online] available at: http://www.endnote.com/, accessed 21.4.11.

Thomson Reuters (2011c) *Social Sciences Citation Index®*, [online] available at: http://thomsonreuters.com/products_services/science/science_products/a-z/social_sciences_citation_index/, accessed 3.5.11.

Thomson Reuters (2011d) *ISI Web of Knowledge™*, [online] available at: http://wokinfo.com/, accessed 8.5.11.

Torrance, H. (2008) Building confidence in qualitative research: engaging the demands of policy, *Qualitative Inquiry*, 14(4): 507–27.

University of Manchester (2011) *Zetoc*, [online] available at: http://zetoc.mimas.ac.uk/, accessed 9.5.11.

University of Nottingham (2010) *The Directory of Open Access Repositories*, [online] available at: http://www.opendoar.org/, accessed 12.4.11.

University of Southampton (2011) *Registry of Open Access Repositories (ROAR)*, [online] available at: http://roar.eprints.org/, accessed 12.4.11.

Van de Werfhorst, H.G. and Luijkx, R. (2010) Educational field of study and social mobility: disaggregating social origin and education, *Sociology*, 44(4): 695–715.

Veltri, B.T. (2008) Teaching or service? The site-based realities of Teach for America teachers in poor, urban schools, *Education and Urban Society*, 40(5): 511–42.

Vongkhamphra, E.G., Davis, C. and Adem, N. (2010) The resettling process: a case study of a Bantu refugee's journey to the USA, *International Social Work*, 54(2): 246–57.

WorldCat® (2011) *WorldCat®*, [online] available at: http://www.worldcat.org/, accessed 29.4.11.

Index